CONTENTS

CHAPTER 1 Culture and Cultural Diversity 2

CHAPTER 2 Language and Language Acquisition 16

The How-To Handbook

Teaching English Language Learners

TERESA WALTER

Longman

Teaching English Language Learners: The How-To Handbook

Pearson Education, 10 Bank Street, White Plains, NY 10606

Vice president, multimedia and skills: Sherry Preiss
Executive editor: Laura Le Dréan
Development manager: Paula H. Van Ells
Senior development editor: Joan Poole
Vice president, director of design and production: Rhea Banker
Director, editorial production: Linda Moser
Director, electronic production: Aliza Greenblatt
Production editor: Lynn Contrucci
Vice president, domestic marketing: Kate McLoughlin
Vice president, international marketing: Bruno Paul
Marketing manager: Alex Rivas Smith
Senior manufacturing buyer: Dave Dickey
Photo research: Tara Maldonado
Cover design: Pat Wosczyk
Text design and composition: Lisa Ghiozzi
Text font: 11/13 Minion
Photo credits: Page 12, Ariel Skelley/CORBIS; page 36, © David Young-Wolff/Photo Edit;
    page 126, © Will Hart

Library of Congress Cataloging-in-Publication Data

Walter, Teresa.
    Teaching English language learners: the how-to handbook / by Teresa Walter.
        p. cm.
    Rev. ed. of: Amazing English! / Teresa Walter. c1996.
    Includes bibliographical references.
    ISBN 0-13-150088-0
1. English language—Study and teaching—Foreign speakers—Handbooks, manuels, etc.
I. Walter, Teresa. Amazing English! II. Title.
PE1128.A2W25 2004
428'.0071—dc22

                                                            2004003640

LONGMAN ON THE **WEB**

Longman.com offers online resources for
teachers and students. Access our Companion
Websites, our online catalog, and our local
offices around the world.

Visit us at **longman.com**.

Printed in the United States of America
    6 7 8 9 10—BAH—09 08 07

To Ed, Mat, and David—my good guys

INTRODUCTION

What do teachers need to know to teach students of English effectively? What are the essential principles that must be known and understood? What are the effective strategies and practices that bring life to these principles and enhance learning opportunities for English language learners? This professional development guide attempts to answer these questions in a practical, straightforward manner. Truly a how-to, it provides an overview of the essential research, key principles, and promising practices that are either cutting edge or have stood the test of time to become foundational truths about language acquisition.

Teaching English Language Learners simplifies the often daunting process of teaching students who do not yet understand the language of instruction. The book is divided into five accessible chapters:

1. Culture and Cultural Diversity
2. Language and Language Acquisition
3. Literacy Development
4. Academic/Content Area Development
5. Assessment and Evaluation

Each chapter begins with a *Preview* in which teachers can assess their prior knowledge and particular interest in the chapter topic. A parallel *Review* section at the end of the chapter enables teachers to assess and apply what they have learned and pinpoint areas of further interest. Throughout the book, marginal tips and notes, charts, and graphic organizers provide additional information and suggestions. Also featured are *Resource Pages, Chapter Notes,* and an extensive *Reference* section at the back of the book.

This book is designed to be a valuable reference tool for a wide variety of teachers and educators. People who would benefit from this book include:

- Student-teachers who are beginning university teacher-training programs
- New teachers who are just starting out in the field
- Experienced teachers who are new to teaching English language learners
- Experienced teachers of English language learners in search of new insights
- Staff developers, professional developers, professors, and other professionals who prepare teachers to better meet the academic needs of English language learners

Teaching English Language Learners expands and updates the information in my previous book, *Amazing English! How-To Handbook.* It is my hope that this book will continue to serve those who serve English. May this book be of value to those entrusted with the amazing task of teaching English language learners.

Teresa Walter

About the Author

Teresa Walter has devoted the majority of her professional life to teaching learners of English. She has taught ESL and bilingual education classes, authored ELD curriculum, and implemented ELD programs. In addition, she has served as a school-site and district-level administrator for English learner support programs in San Diego City Schools in California. She has also conducted numerous professional development and teacher-training courses for teachers at all levels. This book, *Teaching English Language Learners,* is based on her popular professional development book, *Amazing English! How-To Handbook.*

They Don't Prepare Me for This
Mayra Fernández

they don't prepare me for this

a sea of faces so different from my
own mirrored image

some so afraid
of my eyes so large
not almond-shaped
like their beautiful mama's

or of a skin so pale
could she be sick, some must be thinking

but prepared or not
I try

take out your math books, I request
in the Queen's English
isn't math a universal language?
but they sit perfectly still

they don't prepare me for this

so I take a math book
with great flourish point and say MATH BOOK!
immediately 33 math books
are produced

I smile in relief
they smile
in relief

they don't prepare me for this

but I'm gonna try
perhaps I could learn Vietnamese,
Cantonese, Mandarin, Farsi, Korean
and Spanish by Christmas

CHAPTER 1

Culture and Cultural Diversity

> Dean, 16, a Chinese boy from Laos, arrived in San Francisco when he was 10. Like many students . . . he remembered his first day in California schools as if it were today. "The school was so big I didn't know how you were supposed to know where to go, when. There was no one who could speak my language and explain to me. My uncle had told me if I needed any help to go to the Dean. My teacher asked me something and I didn't understand her. So I just said, 'Dean. Dean.'—because I needed help. That is how I got my American name. She was asking me, 'What is your name?' Now everybody calls me Dean. Now it is funny, but it is also sad. My name comes from not knowing what was going on."
>
> —L. Olsen and T. Chen, *The World Enrolls*[1]

Education never takes place in a vacuum. The classroom is a place where people of diverse backgrounds, experiences, cultures, and frequently languages converge for the purpose of learning. The dynamics of this interaction can take many forms, all of which greatly influence schooling. Classroom practices and students' ultimate academic success are largely the result of perceptions of language and culture held by both the teacher and the students.[2]

The context for learning is influenced both by what students bring with them to school and what we provide in schools. Effective instruction requires that we first know and understand our students and then use these understandings to create a climate of respect, support, and expectation.

What do you already KNOW about culture and cultural diversity?

What do you WANT to know or learn?

KNOW THE LEARNER

The first step in planning effective instruction is knowing the learner. Gathering background information on students equips the school and the teacher to better understand and meet the educational needs of their English learners. All students bring with them life experiences that can be used to support them in their new country and in school. We must meet students where they are and start with what they bring.

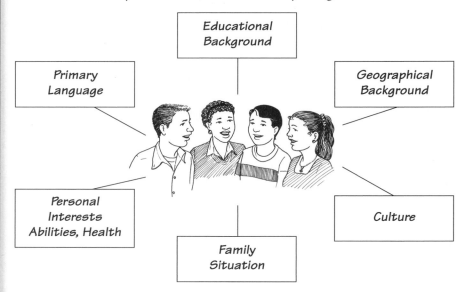

Primary Language

What language or languages are spoken in the home, and in what language does the student function best? In other words, what is the "language of the heart"? To what degree is this primary language developed? What is the level of literacy in this language?

Numerous research studies affirm the idea that success and proficiency in one language directly contribute to success and proficiency in another language.[3] Identify and encourage the further development of the primary language proficiency of students.

What are the primary languages of your students? What is their level of language proficiency in these languages?

Educational Background

Has the student been in school before? If so, to what degree? Is the student receiving additional supplemental educational services provided by the family?

Students who come to us with high levels of education tend to do better than those who have received little or no prior schooling.[4] Educated students (a) have more academic background, language, and conceptual development that transfers to English and (b) are confident learners who bring an attitude of expectation—they *expect* to learn and succeed.

Students transfer not only their primary language literacy and academic skills but also their

How can you help students who have never been in school before or those who have had severely interrupted schooling? How can you help them develop an understanding of school and class procedures such as attendance, lunch, moving between classes, and using the restrooms? How can you teach them to use classroom tools, such as scissors or sharpeners, and organize their school work using binders or folders?

- Perceptions of themselves as learners
- Coping strategies for how to learn
- Skills at socializing[5]

Geographical Background: Immigrant, Refugee, or Native-Born?

What is the country of origin? What are the circumstances of immigration? Was immigration to the United States a conscious choice or necessitated by war or imminent danger or hardship? Was trauma experienced or witnessed prior to or as a part of immigration? Did the student come from a rural or urban area?

It is normal for immigrants, refugees in particular, to go through a period of adjustment, or culture shock, on arriving in the United States and entering its institutions. Background knowledge about the circumstances of immigration helps the school and teacher understand and be sensitive to the issues faced by the new arrivals as well as be proactive in planning and providing needed support or support services.

What are the circumstances of arrival for your students? Encourage them to share their stories with one another.

TIP Have students develop poster reports that describe and/or picture the place of origin, family, significant events, and so on. Students may also bring in significant items or artifacts.

Culture

What is the dominant cultural background of the student and the student's family? What are the basic beliefs concerning education (attendance, roles and responsibilities of teachers, students, and parents), family, friends, conflict resolution, religion, and so on? What are the major important days of celebration?

What cultures are represented in your class? How can you demonstrate that these cultures are valued and respected?

Understanding is based on and begins with respect for and appreciation of individual, family, and cultural diversity. This understanding must extend beyond surface manifestations (holidays, foods) to the deeper elements of culture, such as values and beliefs. Information regarding the background culture of students can be obtained from the students themselves, parents, community organizations and resources, colleagues, and print resources.

Refer to "Understanding Culture," page 6.

Family Situation

What is the family situation? Who is caring for the student? Does anyone in the home speak English? Is the family in the United States permanently or temporarily? Is the family aware of available community resources and services in its home language and culture?

Extreme caution and care should be taken in obtaining information about the family situation. Understandably, families may be reluctant to divulge their life circumstances.

An awareness of family situations helps teachers better understand their students, and it establishes a framework for parent involvement. The context and perceptions students bring with them are rooted in the home. Family factors such as coherence, level of stress, financial situation, and ability to access mainstream American life via language or other resources all contribute to a student's ability to successfully function in school.

What are the family situations of your students? How can you use this information to support both the student and his or her family?

Personal Interests/Abilities/Health

What are the student's special interests, abilities, or talents? Are there any physical or health conditions that influence learning or instruction (vision, hearing, food allergies, and so on)?

Using a student's natural interest or skills in a given area serves as an excellent starting point and vehicle for further learning. It also demonstrates to all around that the student is capable, even if the student cannot yet give voice to these abilities in English. Additionally, it is not uncommon for refugees or immigrants to bring health conditions that may or may not have been properly diagnosed. Identifying and treating these conditions will make a positive impact on learning and adjusting to a new environment.

What are the special talents and abilities of your students? How can you tie this into classroom instruction across the curriculum? Do your students exhibit signs of potential health concerns? Could vision or hearing problems be interfering with comprehension?

Gathering Background Information

Gathering the information can be a challenge and must be done with the utmost respect and care. Recent immigrants or refugees are often reluctant to share personal information—and their preferences must be honored. Possible resources include parents, former teachers, friends, sponsoring agencies (in the case of many refugees or immigrants), community resources, school files and documents, and the students themselves.

It is most helpful to get the information on the same day the student is enrolled, as the family often brings an interpreter. If not, schedule a parent conference as soon as possible.

As students become more comfortable in the new environment and more competent English users, they become one of the best sources of their own histories.

BRAINSTORM
What are some ways that background information will serve a practical purpose in your instruction?

UNDERSTANDING CULTURE

Culture is the way we do things around here.

—Aida Walqui[6]

Students bring with them to the classroom a rich variety of cultural backgrounds. In addressing this diversity, teachers have a twofold responsibility:

- To try to understand and be sensitive to the diverse cultures students bring with them
- To help students understand and adjust to the new culture of which they are now a part

Both of these aspects must be in place for students to feel that what they bring with them is valued and respected, as well as feeling that they fit in and have a place in the new culture. Meaningful appreciation of cultural diversity grows from concrete, positive personal experiences, interactions, and awareness.

Language, used to describe, label, and communicate our world, is intricately tied to culture. Functional aspects of language, such as the meaning given to gestures and body language and the social norms that dictate appropriate language usage, are defined by the culture of the language users. Demonstrating value and respect for an individual's language serves to validate that individual's culture as well.

To be a student of culture, teachers must be patient and observant. Behavior standards are not universal. What is common and expected in one culture may be unacceptable in another. Students who consistently interrupt conversations or hesitate to chime in may be reflecting behavioral norms supported by their home cultures. Body language or nonverbal communication is also culturally based. In some cultures, avoiding eye contact is interpreted as being evasive or apathetic; in others, focusing the eyes downward is seen as the utmost form of respect. Sensitivity, respect,

TIP Consciously model "the way we do things around here." Include procedures, customs, social graces, and so on.

How do you provide ongoing *positive* interactions with your students?

TIP For one day, monitor the nonverbal communication you use in the classroom (shrugging shoulders, pointing, lifting eyebrows, etc.). Focus on helping your English learners understand what these physical actions mean.

Can you think of behaviors that indicate lack of familiarity with American customs or culture or situations in which students are engaging in behaviors not acceptable in this culture?

and knowledge of different cultural expectations will help teachers gain understanding of the students and families they serve and increase the enjoyment of teaching and living in a culturally diverse environment.

Aspects of Culture

Del Hymes identifies the various aspects of culture, listed as follows.[7] Add other examples of culture beneath each heading.

Values and Beliefs
- Family
- Success
- Friendship
- Education
- _____
- _____

Everyday Ways of Doing Things
- Food
- Dress and appearance
- Home routines and chores
- Sense of self and space
- Time and time consciousness
- Rewards and recognition
- _____
- _____

Special Events
- Holidays and related traditional costumes
- Birthdays
- Religious observations/celebrations
- Other celebrations
- _____
- _____

Developing cultural understanding and respect requires us to look beyond special events and everyday ways of doing things toward *values and beliefs*. These intangibles—what is valued and believed—form the heart of culture.

It should be noted that culture is fluid and ever changing. Even in the same region, individual cultural differences are common.

Building Cross-Cultural Skills

Rubin[8] has identified the following attitudes and behaviors as important in building cross-cultural skills.

- *Communicate respect:* Transmit, verbally and nonverbally, positive regard, encouragement, and sincere interest.
- *Be nonjudgmental:* Withhold judgment and remain objective while listening in such a way that the other can fully share the self.
- *Personalize knowledge and perception:* Recognize and communicate that "my" view or perception may not be the only view or perception.
- *Display empathy:* Try to understand situations from another's point of view. Think, feel, and understand from another's perspective.

TIP Find times to teach about the expectations of this culture in ways that are respectful and do not embarrass or degrade. Look for opportunities to develop cultural literacy related to common background knowledge and experiences (for example, the tooth fairy, "The Boy Who Cried Wolf," or "Johnny Appleseed").

What is your personal culture? Beneath each of the headings on the left, list a few items that signify your own personal culture.

Compare your personal culture with others. What are the similarities and differences?

Which elements of your personal culture might be difficult for others to adapt to?

Where are you in the development of your cross-cultural skills? Review each item in Rubin's list and rank yourself as follows:

✓✓✓ Excellent. "I'm there."
✓✓ Pretty good. "I'm on the way."
✓ Needs work. "Where do I begin?"

- *Role flexibility:* Be able to accomplish tasks in a manner and time frame that accommodates the values and concerns of others.
- *Demonstrate reciprocal concern:* Dialog, interact, and actively engage others in the process at hand.
- *Tolerate ambiguity:* Be able to cope with cultural differences and new or unpredictable situations with little visible discomfort or irritation.

 BRAINSTORM
How can you help students build cross-cultural skills?

DEVELOPING A POSITIVE CLASSROOM CLIMATE

I have come to a frightening conclusion. I am the decisive element in the classroom. It is my personal approach that creates the climate. It is my daily mood that makes the weather. As a teacher I possess tremendous power to make a child's life miserable or joyous. I can be a tool of torture or an instrument of inspiration. I can humiliate or humor, hurt or heal. In all situations it is my response that decides whether crisis will be escalated or de-escalated, and a child humanized or dehumanized.

—Haim Ginott, *Between Teacher and Child*[9]

Teachers are given a great opportunity to positively affect the lives of their students. Day by day, interaction by interaction, teachers can employ cross-cultural skills to build a classroom climate of respect, validation, and expectation. This climate directly impacts student success.

When students feel that they have a place, they will learn. Providing appropriate models and engaging students in positive interactions from day one promotes a positive classroom climate. Aida Walqui proposed the following model that illustrates the interplay among the various cultures to which students belong and the climates in which they daily interact.

CULTURAL CONTEXTS
Each context has its own culture and climate.

Think about your students. What "worlds" do they walk through each day? How different is the culture of your classroom from the culture of the school? their family? the immediate community? society at large?

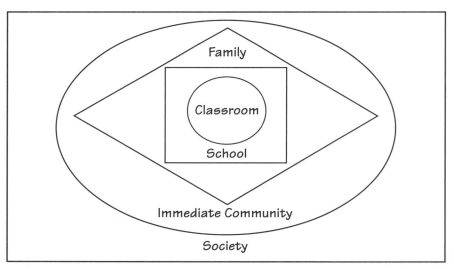

—Adapted from Walqui, 1995.

Each area has its own culture and climate. For example, the culture of some families may be similar, but each family has its own unique climate. It is common for a mismatch to occur from layer to layer. Demonstrating cultural sensitivity and understanding and explicitly acknowledging, "What we do here may be different from . . . ," helps to prepare and equip students to face these inevitable differences. As Aida Walqui tells her students, "You must have the strength to face it."

THE HIDDEN CURRICULUM

For children to learn, they need to feel respected and valued. When attention is given to creating a classroom environment and organization where this happens, the conditions for learning are established.

—Leanna Traill[10]

What are the things you do to create a supportive classroom culture and climate that supports students, maintains high expectations, yet recognizes the diverse backgrounds and daily experiences of each student?

Some of the most powerful factors contributing to classroom climate come from what Leanna Traill calls "The Hidden Curriculum." This hidden curriculum is rarely studied, publicized, or evaluated, yet it pervades all aspects of classroom life:

Reflect on your teaching and classroom climate. Identify your "hidden curriculum" and the ways in which you demonstrate respect and value.

- *Attitudes:* Knowingly or unknowingly, the attitudes of the teacher are immediately transmitted to students. Teachers must, therefore, actively demonstrate positive attitudes regarding diversity, developing positive self-esteem, encouraging positive interactions, and promoting multi-language use.
- *Environment:* Everything in the classroom sends a message to students. The environment must be student-centered, recognizing and promoting the languages and cultures students bring with them. Students should feel at home in the classroom and see that their work is valued and displayed. Materials reflecting the students' backgrounds should be integral to the room, and furniture should be situated to encourage interaction and use.
- *Materials:* Materials should reflect the classroom population and other cultures as well. Students should have access to materials about their countries of origin, immediate communities, and topics of interest and to the extent possible, resources in their primary language. Students should be encouraged to bring in additional relevant resources.
- *Classroom organization:* Classroom organization should permit flexibility for varied student interactions (pairs, cooperative/collaborative groups, and so on) and grouping configurations (such as primary language, heterogeneous, and flexible focus groups).
- *Topic relevance:* Topics should relate to student background, experiences, and immediate needs.

It mattered to one . . .

Reflect and then describe one instance in which *you* made a difference in the life of one student.

What have you done that leads to student empowerment? Record your own successes for each category: cultural/language incorporation, home-school interactions, instructional practices, and assessment.

EMPOWERMENT

One day in Hawaii a ferocious storm washed hundreds of starfish ashore. A woman, on her morning walk, bent down every few steps to throw a starfish back into the sea. A man saw her and commented, "There are so many of the poor things it can't make any real difference for you to throw these few back." With a knowing smile, she tossed another starfish into the water and turning to the man said, "It made a difference to this one."

—Sue Patton Thoele, *Making a Difference*[11]

The Power of Individual Interactions

James Cummins has developed a model that demonstrates how educational institutions (schools) can systematically empower or disable English learners.[12] Central to this model is the idea that teachers have the personal power to either empower or disable individual students in the personal and individual interactions that occur day after day. These interactions, when combined with interactions with others representing the "institutions of society," serve to construct, in the minds of students, a perceived view of themselves as learners and their place in school and society at large. It is this perception that in effect enables or disables.

Cummins advocates the adoption of principles and practices that serve to empower rather than disable students. These principles and practices follow, along with specific implementation strategies and tips.

- *Cultural/language incorporation:* Use and development of the primary language is encouraged and supported. Language and culture are viewed as tools to make meaning of content and facilitate learning. Signs, notices, newsletters, and so on incorporate the home language.
- *Home-school interactions:* Parents are involved as partners and work collaboratively with teachers to provide education in the home and school. Regular home-school communication occurs, and parents are invited to observe and participate in classroom and school events.
- *Instructional practices:* Teachers engage students in tasks that encourage and enable them to become generators of their own knowledge. Instruction is student-centered, with students taking increasing responsibility to interact and use language to express ideas, engage in discourse, negotiate for meaning, and control their own learning.
- *Assessment:* Teachers and schools become advocates for students, seeking to genuinely assist students rather than using (inappropriate) assessment tools to legitimize the location of the problem as being in the student. Student knowledge is assessed in a variety of ways, and teachers become "kid watchers," constantly monitoring learning and adapting instruction to match what students need.

EMPOWERING THE LANGUAGE MINORITY STUDENT IN AN ENGLISH-DOMINANT CLASSROOM

◆ Reflect the various cultural groups in the school district by providing signs in the main office and elsewhere that welcome people in the different languages of the community.

◆ Encourage students to use the primary language (L1) around the school.

◆ Provide opportunities for students from the same ethnic group to communicate with one another in their L1 where possible (for example, in cooperative learning groups on at least some occasions).

◆ Recruit people who can tutor students in their L1.

◆ Provide books written in the various languages in both classrooms and the school library.

◆ Incorporate greetings and information in the various languages in newsletters and other official school communications.

◆ Provide bilingual and/or multilingual signs.

◆ Display the pictures and objects of the various cultures represented at the school.

◆ Create units of work that incorporate other languages in addition to the school language.

◆ Encourage students to write contributions in their L1 for school newspapers and magazines.

◆ Provide opportunities for students to study their L1 in elective subjects and/or in extracurricular clubs.

◆ Encourage parents to help in the classroom, library, playground, and in clubs.

◆ Invite second-language learners to use their L1 during assemblies, prize giving, and other official functions.

◆ Invite people from ethnic minority communities to act as resource people and to speak to students in both formal and informal settings.

From *Empowering Minority Students* by James Cummins, © 1989.
Reprinted by permission.

Refer to page 11 for a list of suggestions for empowering English learners, even if you don't speak their home language.

The dilemma for many teachers is "How can I support and validate the languages and cultures of the students in my multilanguage classroom when I speak only English?" The answer lies in consciously adopting strategies and practices that empower rather than disable students: know the learner, understand the culture and develop cross-cultural skills, create a positive classroom climate, and incorporate Cummins's empowerment principles and practices.

FAMILY AND COMMUNITY RESOURCES

Promoting Parents as Partners

Teachers and parents share similar goals regarding the students they jointly serve. They must, therefore, work as partners to bring together the two worlds of home and school and help the individual student learn and grow. Teachers and schools must initiate contact and take action to involve parents. Suggestions for parent involvement include the following:

- Make home visits. Home visits give valuable cultural information and insight, help parents and students feel more comfortable with teacher and school, and give ideas for parent involvement.
- Attend community/cultural celebrations.
- Learn about the traditions and beliefs of parents.
- Trust parents to help at home. The development of ideas, concepts, and processes can be done in any language.
- Confer with parents. Formal and informal conferences provide opportunities for teachers and parents to share information and insights about the student. Provide interpreters.
- Take specific action to involve parents. Invite them to visit your classroom. Make personal contacts in the home language. Listen to parents' ideas and suggestions. Encourage action and be prepared to follow their lead.

- Communicate with parents on a regular basis in their home language.
- Expect parents to be involved, and provide the support (interpreters, child care, transportation, and so on) that will enable them to be involved.

 BRAINSTORM
What other specific strategies, activities, or techniques have you used to establish and develop positive home-school connections?

Which strategies do you think would be the most effective with your student and parent population?

Demonstrating Support for Families

To demonstrate support for parents, elevate their "status" in the following ways:

- Avoid using students as interpreters for their parents. This shifts the power from parents to their children, thereby robbing parents of their parental authority.
- Use parents as cultural and subject-matter experts. Invite them as guest speakers to share experiences and/or expertise with the class.
- Encourage the continued development of the primary language in the home. Benefits include the development of language and concepts and continued nurturing and development of important family relationships.
- Understand and be supportive of home culture and family structure, including roles and responsibilities and forms of discipline.

Identifying and Utilizing Community Resources

Most communities have a variety of agencies—both private and public—that serve new immigrants and English language learners. Possible community resources include refugee centers, sponsoring agencies (specific to immigrant population), state and federal relief agencies, religious institutions, private schools, embassies, and key community leaders.

 BRAINSTORM
What additional resources are available in your school district, community, or city?

REVIEW

Refer to and review the Preview page for this chapter (page 3). Was your prior knowledge accurate? (Did you have any misconceptions or inaccurate ideas?)

What did you LEARN about culture and cultural diversity?

How can you apply this information? (Include one or two specific ideas.)

What else do you want to know?

NOTES

CHAPTER 2

Language and Language Acquisition

> Children are seekers of meaning. No sooner do they learn how to talk than they begin asking questions about simple things as well as about the dilemmas of human existence that have perplexed philosophers and theologians from the dawn of time.
>
> —California Department of Education, *It's Elementary*[1]

As human beings, we have a need to make meaning of our surroundings. Anyone, when placed in a new situation, immediately tries to sort it out, tying the unknown to the known. This is true for English learners placed in an all-English classroom. They immediately seek out clues to "crack the code" of the classroom. Visuals, gestures, a friendly face—all help students create meaning of the new environment.

It is this need to make meaning that is at the heart of language acquisition. As students continue to make and negotiate meaning through relevant interactions and activities, language is acquired at increasingly higher levels. The goal, then, for students receiving English language development (ELD) is that they be able to use language to communicate effectively and appropriately for all life's requirements, both social and academic.

What do you already KNOW about language and language acquisition?

What do you WANT to know or learn?

What is language? Reflect, and then record your own definition of language.

Note: The terms *English as a second language (ESL)* and *English language development (ELD),* although distinguished by some, are used interchangeably in this handbook. They both refer to the development of English proficiency (in all its domains, through nativelike proficiency) by students who speak a primary language other than English.

PRINCIPLES OF LANGUAGE

From the abundance of current research in the field of language and language acquisition, some basic principles have emerged:

Language is functional.
Language has use and function in real-world interactions. Language has purpose and function and is acquired through meaningful use and interaction.

Language and culture are interrelated.
Language patterns and use are different in different cultures. These variations reflect the cultural norms, values, and beliefs of a culture. To learn language is to learn culture.

Language varies and changes.
Language use varies according to person, situation, and purpose. Language also varies by region, social class, and ethnic group and changes over time to adapt to the ever-changing needs of the language users.

Language skills develop interdependently.
Authentic language use often requires the simultaneous use of several language domains.

Native language proficiency contributes to second language acquisition.
Proficiency in the native language directly affects a person's ability to efficiently acquire both social and academic aspects of a second language.

COMMUNICATIVE COMPETENCE

It is not enough to be able to read, write, and understand basic language. One must be able to use language to get things done. Communicative competence, a term developed by Del Hymes, is defined as the ability to use language appropriately in a variety of contexts. This involves not only employing accurate forms of language but also knowing the social rules of use that determine what language is appropriate to specific situations.[2] Additional research has contributed to an understanding of communicative competence that incorporates the following four essential elements.[3]

ELEMENTS OF COMMUNICATIVE COMPETENCE

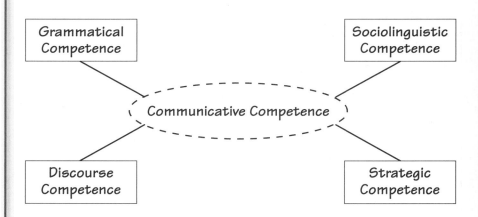

1. Grammatical Competence

Grammatical competence focuses on "correctness" and accuracy—on the skills necessary to speak and write accurately, to know the language code (vocabulary, grammar, pronunciation, spelling, and so on).

2. Sociolinguistic Competence

Sociolinguistic competence involves the appropriate use of language in varied social settings. It takes into account factors such as social norms, status of the participants, and other rules or social conventions that influence both meaning and form, such as knowing how to request information, accept or refuse assistance, and other "social graces" expected of competent users of the language ("Excuse me, can I borrow your pen?").

3. Discourse Competence

Discourse competence is the ability to appropriately use cohesion devices and coherent rules to engage in conversations requiring the combining and connecting of phrases and sentences. This competence requires the participant to be both a sender and receiver of language, alternating the roles appropriately in conversations or written discourse.

4. Strategic Competence

Strategic competence involves the manipulation of language, both verbal and nonverbal, to achieve the communication goals. This competence is utilized for two major reasons:

- To clarify meaning (paraphrasing an idea, searching for a word, gesturing to convey meaning)
- To enhance communication (emphasizing a specific word, using body language, changing voice tone or volume for effect)

Competent users of language must be proficient in appropriately using all aspects of communicative competence. English language development programs should focus on developing all aspects of communicative competence, resulting in students who are truly proficient users of English, able to use English for all life's requirements, both social and academic.

BRAINSTORM
How can you model and teach each aspect of communicative competence?

If communicative competence is the goal, what types of language-learning experiences must students engage in?

Refer to Chapter 3, page 71, for more on cohesion and cohesive devices.

Think of one student. What aspects of communicative competence are the most developed? What aspects need more focused attention?

LANGUAGE AND CONTEXT: LANGUAGE REGISTER

While cultures may share many common purposes for using language, how these things actually get done varies from culture to culture.

—Pauline Gibbons, *Scaffolding Language, Scaffolding Learning*[4]

Language is influenced by many factors. One of the most subtle yet influential factors is *context*. Context can be thought of in two ways: cultural context and situational context.

Cultural context reflects the ways in which speakers within a culture "agree" to do things. Language exchanges such as greetings and good-byes, ordering food at a restaurant, or writing business and personal letters are examples of shared cultural knowledge.

Situational context refers to the ways in which language varies according to the context of the situation. Situational context is influenced by what is being talked/written about, the relationship between the speakers/reader or writer, and whether the language is spoken or written.[5] The situational context of language use is also referred to as language *register*.

Language register changes when the situation or context in which it was produced is changed. As language moves away from face-to-face, here-and-now conversations, it must become more explicit because it can't depend on shared experience to carry meaning. For this reason, writing generally requires a more formal (and academic) language register. The writer must carefully construct the context that is not seen by the reader to convey meaning.

Pauline Gibbons provides the following example of students' situational language use:

1. *Look, it's making them move. Those don't stick.*
   [Small group of students. Context is here-and-now. Need to be there to understand references.]

2. *We found out the pins stuck on the magnet.*
   [Recounting experience to the teacher. Reference is now to specific objects.]

3. *Our experiment showed that magnets attract some metals.*
   [Written summary. A general, more academic account. Specific terms, such as "attract" instead of "stick."]

4. *Magnetic attraction occurs only between ferrous metals.*
   [Definition from a student encyclopedia. Denser language and the process is summarized.][6]

The register of each line changed because the context in which it was produced was different. The lines became increasingly more explicit and formal as the situation moved from the here-and-now with peers and a spoken interaction with the teacher to a written summary of the experiment and finally to a formal written definition.

Language register is also a part of sociolinguistic competence. Refer to the section on sociolinguistic competence on page 19.

Comments such as "Hand me that thing" or "It's over there" are understood only in a shared here-and-now context.

1. Informal register.

2. Slightly more formal—but simple language.

3. More formal—using academic language.

4. Very formal—dense academic language.

Note the increasing academic demands placed on students as the context shifts to writing.

ACADEMIC REQUIREMENTS OF LANGUAGE

Related to the idea of communicative competence is Cummins's definition of two levels of language proficiency: basic interpersonal communication skills (BICS) and cognitive academic language proficiency (CALP).[7] Cummins notes that many misconceptions about students' abilities, capabilities, and even basic intelligence are related to the way in which "language proficiency" has been defined. Specifically, students' conversational fluency in English is often (mistakenly) taken as a reflection of their overall proficiency in the language. To address these misconceptions, Cummins clarifies "the fundamental distinction between conversational and academic aspects of language proficiency."[8]

BICS Basic interpersonal communication skills involve using language for social, face-to-face, everyday situations. BICS tends to be very contextualized, providing abundant clues to comprehension. It refers to basic fluency in the language, and it is something students acquire relatively quickly, usually within two years.

CALP Cognitive academic language proficiency involves language skills and functions of an academic or cognitive nature. This is the language needed to accomplish academic tasks. There are fewer context clues, and students must draw meaning from the language itself. CALP typically takes much longer to acquire, usually about four to seven years.

You May Have Heard . . .

You may have heard teachers at your school saying, "Why does he still need English language instruction? He speaks English very well. Listen to him talking to his friends at lunch. He talks all the time." When asked how the student is functioning academically, the response is, "He's below grade level and not doing well, but the problem must be something other than language." This student has acquired BICS—conversational fluency—but has not yet achieved CALP—full academic language proficiency in English. What he needs is more time for focused academic language development.

In school contexts, students must utilize CALP as well as BICS to succeed academically. Students who appear to have achieved nativelike conversational skills in English may take several years before they match their native-English-speaking peers in academic English. This is largely because English speakers are also developing their language proficiency at the same time. In essence, we're aiming at a moving target and must provide accelerated instruction for English language learners to close the gap.

CALP, however, is highly transferable from one language to another. If you have cognitive proficiency in one language, you simply need to acquire the matching language labels for these ideas in a second language for transfer to occur. This common underlying proficiency explains why we don't need to relearn cognitive tasks or academic subjects such as math and science in a new language.[9]

BRAINSTORM
What evidence have you seen or heard of your students using BICS? CALP?

BICS and CALP

Think back. Can you think of an instance when a student seemed to be fluent in English yet had difficulty in the academic areas of the curriculum?

Do you think this was a case in which the student needed more time and focused academic language development (CALP)? Why do/don't you think so?

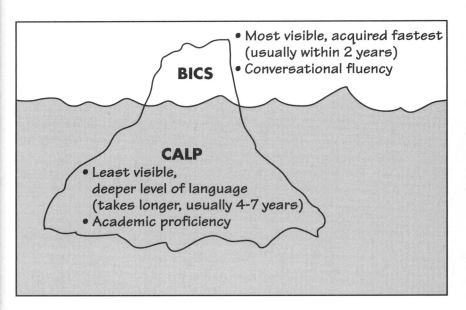

- Most visible, acquired fastest (usually within 2 years)
- Conversational fluency

BICS

CALP
- Least visible, deeper level of language (takes longer, usually 4-7 years)
- Academic proficiency

Refer to page 23 for an annotated example of the quadrants.

Cummins further defines the dimensions of social and academic language by looking at tasks in terms of cognitive demands and contextual clues. The context of a task can range along a continuum from context embedded (lots of clues) to context reduced (no context clues).[10] Similarly, tasks range from cognitively undemanding (easy) to cognitively demanding (hard). The continuums are presented in a model in which they intersect and form quadrants with varying levels of supports and challenges. To achieve academically, students must be able to accomplish tasks at all levels. Cummins's quadrants are useful in identifying the levels of proficiency required for specific tasks and promoting the use of strategies that help support students in constructing meaning from more academically challenging tasks.

In which of Cummins's quadrants (on page 23) should instruction begin for students at the earliest stages of language proficiency? Why?

BRAINSTORM
What other classroom activities fit into each of Cummins's quadrants?

LANGUAGE AND CONTENT ACTIVITIES
WITHIN CUMMINS'S QUADRANTS

Cognitively Undemanding (Easy)

A	C
• Developing survival vocabulary • Following demonstrated directions • Playing simple games • Engaging in face-to-face interactions • Participating in art, music, and physical education	• Engaging in telephone conversations • Reading and writing for personal purposes: notes, lists, sketches, and so on
B	**D**
• Participating in hands-on science and mathematics activities • Making maps, models, charts, and graphs • Solving math computational problems • Making brief oral presentations • Understanding academic presentations through the use of visuals, demonstrations, active participation, realia, and so on • Understanding written texts through discussion, illustrations, and visuals • Writing academic reports with the aid of outlines, structures, and so on	• Understanding academic presentations without visuals or demonstrations: lectures • Making formal oral presentations • Solving math word problems without illustrations • Writing compositions, essays, and research reports in content areas • Reading for information in content areas • Taking standardized achievement tests

Context-Embedded (Clues) ← → **Context-Reduced (No Clues)**

Cognitively Demanding (Hard)

—Adapted from Chamot and O'Malley, 1987; and Cummins, 2000, 1981.

HOW DOES THE PRIMARY LANGUAGE INFLUENCE THE ACQUISITION OF ENGLISH?

How can you utilize the students' primary language(s) in the classroom?

As noted, knowledge transfers between languages. "The more I know in my primary language, the more I'll know in a new language." And similarly, "As I learn new things in my new language, I also know it in my home language." It makes a great deal of sense to recognize the huge resource students have in the form of their home language and to do everything possible to encourage the development and enrichment of every student's primary language. This can be accomplished in several ways.

Provide primary language instruction.

This strategy is particularly useful for students in the earlier stages of English language development. Providing primary language instruction and support in core curricular areas allows students to develop (and keep up) academically while also investing in their future success in English. It allows students to immediately engage in the intellectual work of school.

Encourage primary language development at home.

How else can you promote the development of students' primary languages?

This strategy produces a twofold benefit:

- Concepts and ideas continue to be developed in the primary language, enriching the primary language and future success in English.
- Parents and students continue to communicate meaningfully. [11]

Welcome the use of the primary language.

Make opportunities for students to work in primary language clusters to clarify ideas and concepts. Demonstrate that you value the language they bring with them. Then have students explain their thinking/conversation in English, providing support as needed.

A student's primary language serves as the foundation on which English proficiency is built. A primary language that is developed and maintained serves to enhance English language development and success in school. The situation should never exist in which students or staff must choose one language and exclude the other.

STAGES OF LANGUAGE PROFICIENCY

Observe your students. In what stages of language proficiency are they?

Is this consistent with the time they have spent learning and practicing English (see the graph on page 25)?

What strategies do you use to further language development?

As students acquire a second language, they progress through a series of predictable stages, similar to first language acquisition. [12] By interacting with and observing students, we can identify their stages of language proficiency. Combining this knowledge with what we already know about the students, we can plan appropriate instruction.

Although students usually progress through the stages in order, they do not always progress at the same rate of speed, nor are each of the stages of equal duration. For example, the beginning stage typically takes less time than other stages, and the intermediate stage can last a couple of years. The accompanying graph illustrates the approximate amount of time needed to progress through the stages of language proficiency. Note that the time frames are very general. Individuals will need varying amounts of time to learn English depending on many factors such as prior education and academic achievement. [13]

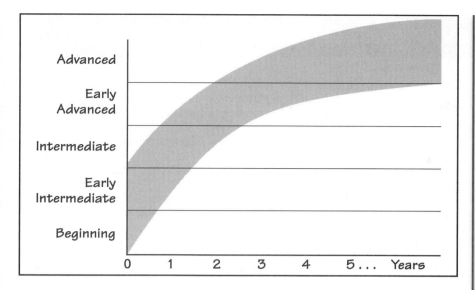

STAGES OF LANGUAGE PROFICIENCY

Refer to page 26 for the stages of language proficiency and instructional strategies appropriate to each stage.

Note that students in advanced fluency are approaching nativelike fluency in English. They are refining and fine-tuning their English. Research indicates that even with good instruction, it may take students four to seven years to reach full proficiency in English.[14]

It should be noted that the stages of language acquisition identified in the graph provide one but certainly not the only way of identifying language development. The stages do prove useful, however, in planning appropriate standards-based programs and instructional activities, as well as in understanding the student characteristics and linguistic behaviors that are typical as students acquire English.[15]

HOW IS LANGUAGE ACQUIRED?

Prior knowledge is the strongest predictor of a student's ability to make inferences about text.

—California Department of Education[16]

Research confirms that language acquisition is enhanced when:

Attention is given to background knowledge and experience.

"Familiarity breeds understanding." There is extensive research that indicates that activiating students' prior knowledge and experience and then giving them ample opportunities to describe and discuss the experiences are highly effective strategies for developing understanding and promoting academic achievement.[17] Students connect and apply what they already know to new learning, making new learning more efficient as new concepts are integrated into existing knowledge or schemata. Further, activating and elaborating on prior knowledge and experience allow the teacher to do the following:

- Identify and supply relevant concepts or language.
- Know and understand the students better.
- Validate students' experience and cultural knowledge, thereby motivating even greater class participation and interaction.

How do you promote language acquisition through familiarity?

IDENTIFYING AND DEVELOPING LANGUAGE PROFICIENCY

Beginning Stage

Student Behavior

- May not yet produce speech or are just beginning to put words together.
- Listen and begin to respond by using nonverbal signals.
- Internalize significant pieces of information.
- Participate through physical actions.
- Respond with one or two words.
- Attend to hands-on demonstrations with greater comprehension.
- Initiate conversations by pointing and using single words.
- Respond nonverbally to a wider range of language input.
- Exhibit no or very limited use of full sentences—very limited fluency.
- Write isolated words or one- to three-word phrases with illustrations.
- Write for self—little or no sense of audience, purpose, or personality.
- Do not yet apply conventions of grammar or word order.

Instruction

- Provide comprehensible input/abundant context clues using visuals, realia, manipulatives, gestures, and so on.
- Model all expected behavior.
- Encourage students to follow simple directions involving physical actions.
- Encourage students to join in group songs, chants, recitations, and so on.
- Assist in developing phonemic awareness.
- Encourage students to participate in role-playing activities.
- Check comprehension frequently.
- Maintain a consistent daily schedule with regular routines to facilitate comprehension.
- Use questioning strategies eliciting one or two words such as

    Yes/No Questions:
    Descriptive: *Is this a _____?*
    Predictable: *Will her aunt come home?*
    Generalizations: *Does the sun ever shine at night?*
    Referential: *Did you like the story?*

    Either/Or Questions:
    Is this a _____ or a _____?
    Do you like _____ or _____?

    "Wh" Questions:
    What color is the _____?
    When do you get here?
    Who ate the _____?

- Expect students to speak English.

Early Intermediate Stage

Student Behavior

- Begin speaking in phrases and short sentences.
- Use speech that sounds telegraphic: *I go home now.*
- Make many errors of grammar and syntax as they experiment with language.
- Communicate central idea but usually lack full development.
- Use some vocabulary from various content areas.
- Writing is usually a loose collection of sentences that reveal limited mastery of English word order.
- Write for themselves but begin to express their own personality and personal thoughts.
- Approximate spelling of words.
- Errors often obscure meaning—verbally and in writing.

Instruction

- Continue providing comprehensible input and contextualizing instruction.
- Ask questions requiring expanded responses.
- Ask more referential questions:
    What would you do if _____?
    What else might happen?
- Provide opportunities for students to engage in social and academic conversations.
- Provide age-appropriate instruction in English language conventions, grammar, and structure.
- Provide feedback and model appropriately when errors are made.
- Provide focused, small-group ELD instruction each day.
- Utilize Specially Designed Academic Instruction in English (SDAIE) strategies.
- Expect students to speak English.

Intermediate Stage

Student Behavior

- Exhibit a command of conversational English and engage in conversations that produce more complex sentences and narratives.

Instruction

- Continue to use strategies from earlier stages, such as contextualization, modeling, demonstrations, and comprehension checks.

Intermediate Stage (continued)

Student Behavior	Instruction

• Increasingly use English related to academic tasks.
• Express more complex thoughts, although may rely heavily on familiar phrases or vocabulary.
• Speech and grammatical errors may still be common but rarely obscure meaning.
• Possess sufficient vocabulary to demonstrate critical thinking in all domains of language.
• Writing conveys complex meaning and detail using simple forms.
• Sentences are mostly simple but usually complete with some variation in structure and are usually in the past or present tense.
• Writing may include loosely connected sentences but there is evidence of emerging fluency.
• Writing demonstrates an audience beyond self but may lack clarity.
• Writing may lack sufficient elaboration.
• Usually spell commonly used words correctly and exhibit increasing command of basic writing conventions such as capitalization and periods.
	• Model standard language structures.
	• Continue building phonemic awareness, emphasizing specific sounds/structures as needed (e.g., plural "s").
	• Ask questions that require phrase and sentence responses.
	• Expand student responses through modeling and extending conversations:
	   Tell me more about _____?
	   I understand, keep going.
	   Why do you think _____?
	• Avoid overt error correction, but model standard usage and continue to provide instruction on language conventions.
	• Provide frequent shared, modeled, and independent writing experiences.
	• View every content lesson as a language lesson, looking for language development opportunities.
	• Engage students in increasingly longer and deeper conversations.
	• Expect students to speak English.

Early Advanced Stage

Student Behavior	Instruction
• Communicate effectively in most formal and informal settings. • Sustain conversations and respond in more complex sentences with greater detail. • Speech and grammatical errors still occur but rarely interfere with communication. • Approach grade-level standards in reading and writing. • Rely heavily on context and prior knowledge to obtain meaning from print but apply with increasing consistency appropriate English usage to a wide variety of literacy needs. • Vocabulary use and writing usually demonstrate understanding of audience and purpose. • Writing demonstrates evidence of purposeful organization and elaboration of central idea, incident, or problem. • Generally fluent but still acquiring irregular and more complex words and sentence structures.	• Continue to engage students and use SDAIE strategies from earlier stages, such as contextualization, modeling, demonstrations, and comprehension checks. • Model and teach increasingly complex English language structures. • Provide instruction that requires students to use English in cognitively demanding situations. • Establish a climate in which students are free to take risks and are supported in their attempts at increasingly higher forms of English. • Immerse students in the genre they are studying, using content as an opportunity for vocabulary and schema building. • Provide and support students through complex, grade-level reading and writing. • Expect students to speak, read, and write in English—supporting them as needed.

Advanced Stage

Student Behavior	Instruction
• Possess the depth of language necessary to meet grade-level standards in all subject areas. • Have full command of conversational English and utilize language related to academic tasks approximating that of native speakers of English. • Comprehend general and implied meaning including figurative and idiomatic language. • Initiate and negotiate conversations using appropriate discourse, and varied grammatical structures and vocabulary. • Pronunciation, intonation, grammar, and word order approximate that of native speakers of English. • Reading and writing, including writing conventions, organization, and purpose, are grade-level appropriate.	• Continue providing targeted instruction according to specific students' needs. • Provide opportunities for further language enhancement and refinement. • Continue with complex and varied literacy tasks. • Continue to maintain high expectations for students and provide instruction commensurate with these expectations.

When requisite background knowledge is lacking, greater time and effort must be spent to build and expand background.

It is also important to note that students with strong educational backgrounds tend to acquire language faster and at higher levels than do their less educationally advantaged peers.[18] This primary language background knowledge transfers to English, making instruction in English more understandable and meaningful.

The context and language are real and purposeful.

Students acquire language when they use it for real purposes. The language used must be relevant, meaningful, and authentic and embedded in a context that makes sense to students.

As students are actively engaged in authentic tasks, they are using language to accomplish a specific purpose, exchange information, or solve a problem that is of interest and relevance to them. The focus of this engagement is on the functional aspect of language (getting things done) rather than its form (grammatical structures). The result is both language and cognitive development.[19]

Language is made comprehensible.

Language is acquired when messages are understood.[20] Students must understand the intent of the message, not necessarily every word that is spoken. This understanding is not based solely on words. Students also obtain meaning from such things as context, visuals, body language, and real objects and interactions.

Krashen suggests that language acquisition is the result of receiving these understandable messages, or "comprehensible input." Comprehensible input connects the known to the unknown and enables students to comprehend more than they can produce ("input + 1"), actually propelling them to higher levels of language proficiency.

Students feel free to take risks.

Students acquire language when they are engaged in meaningful activities and their anxiety level is low. The classroom must be a safe and supportive environment in which students feel free to take risks and recognize that these risks will be rewarded. All students' attempts at language use are encouraged and the teacher steps in with specific language supports when needed to ensure comprehension, further language development, and success. Although there may be some anxiety, the expectation on the part of the teacher and students alike is that students can and will accomplish the task.

Interaction is high.

A wide range of research affirms the idea that active participation and student interaction increases learning and promotes student achievement.[21] This is particularly true for English learners, as highly interactive activities or tasks provide experiences that are both cognitively demanding and contextually supported. Further, research confirms that language development is promoted through interaction and talk.[22] *Language must be used to be acquired.* Communicative interaction and the negotiation of meaning between users of the target language are essential to the process of acquiring language. Interaction and talk are at the heart of the learning process.

As students engage in conversation, they must negotiate meaning through talk so that each understands the intent of the other. Students must at times question, repeat, rephrase, or restate to provide messages

How do you use context, comprehensible input, support, and interaction to promote language acquisition?

Refer to page 33 for techniques on providing comprehensible input.

that are understandable to others. This "comprehensible output" is learned and developed through use. Communicative interaction is the negotiation of meaning through conversations as well as written texts.[23]

Students should be given opportunities throughout each day to use language and interact with a variety of English speakers for a variety of purposes. For example, students should interact:

- With a variety of English-speaking models
- With large groups, small groups, and partners
- Within collaborative and cooperative groups
- Within various language-grouping configurations:

    Primary language: To clarify ideas, concepts, vocabulary

    English learner: To modify or "shelter" instruction or preview/review a lesson

    Heterogeneous groups: For cooperative/collaborative activities, discussions, or learning centers

Note: The effective language classroom will probably not be a quiet one!

Active Listening

Listening, like reading, is an active process. Listening involves comprehension and the active construction of meaning.[24] To acquire language, students at all proficiency levels must be actively engaged. Even students at the beginning levels of proficiency can participate through active listening. They watch, follow, and approximate the actions and language around them.

Active listening continues to be an important strategy for language development as students progress to higher levels of English language proficiency. At these levels, meaning often hinges on subtle references or unfamiliar terms.

The Chinese character for "listen" is composed of four parts.

- *Ears:* To hear the words, tone, and language
- *Eyes:* To see meaning through expression and gestures
- *Undivided attention:* To give respect to the speaker
- *Heart:* To give oneself to understanding

To truly hear, students must give their undivided attention and listen with their ears, eyes, and heart.

High Levels of Expectation

Students will acquire language when the teacher and the students clearly identify the expectation of success. Students are encouraged, supported, and *required* to use language and engage in learning at increasingly higher levels. Statements such as the following reflect the idea that students are expected to take on the language and become increasingly responsible for their own learning.

- *I understand, keep going.*
- *Do you mean _____? OK, this is how you say it. _____. You try.*
- *You're doing great. Tell me more.*

Refer to Chapter 4, page 102, for more information on grouping and collaborative/cooperative learning.

TIP Use "barrier" activities to promote active listening and authentic language. Place a divider (e.g., a screen) between two students. Each student has a set of identical materials (e.g., pictures cards, manipulatives, or story sequencing cards). One arranges the items and then describes the arrangement for the other to replicate. Both negotiate meaning until they are confident that they have the same arrangement. Lift the divider and compare.

TO LISTEN

Ears
Eyes
Undivided Attention
Heart

Let's compare:

A 5-year-old is considered proficient in the language when he or she can speak comparably to another typical 5-year-old native speaker. A 13-, 17-, or 21-year-old, however, is considered proficient when he or she can speak, read, and write comparably not to a 5-year-old but to another 13-, 17-, or 21-year-old native speaker. To be considered proficient in a language, much more is required of older students.

Personality

Personality traits such as shyness, risk-taking behavior, inhibitions, and confidence influence interaction and language acquisition.

Age

Students of all ages can and do acquire language. Current research shows, however, that older children and adults may acquire language faster than young children,[25] perhaps because cognitive/academic proficiency is more fully developed in the primary language of older students. Also, older students bring with them their age-level knowledge of the world, their experience and skills, and their self-perceptions as learners.[26] Younger, preadolescent students have an advantage in at least one aspect of language acquisition: they are more likely than their older counterparts to develop nativelike pronunciation skills.

Attitudes

Student attitudes can have an enormous effect—either positive or negative—on second language acquisition. It is important for learning a new language to be viewed as an additive process—adding a new language to one that has represented life and home—rather than a replacement process—replacing (and devaluing) the home language.[27] Students' positive or negative attitudes in areas such as the ones that follow will influence their willingness to fully invest themselves in acquiring all aspects of a new language.[28]

- *Attitudes toward self:* Self-esteem, self-confidence, and self-perceptions regarding one's ability to learn in general.
- *Attitudes toward language and those who speak it:* Largely shaped by experiences and interactions with those close by. Negative or positive attitudes (regarding both the first and second language) rub off as a result of firsthand experience, or the strong influence of peers or family members.
- *Attitudes toward the teacher and the classroom environment:* Largely the result of personal or family experiences in school. Positive and negative experiences facilitate the development of strong attitudes that either encourage students to fully participate in the school experience—including acquiring English, the language of school—or create in students a feeling of alienation, leading to ambivalent feelings toward English and education.

Note that attitudes are largely based on experience, either personal experience or the experiences of those who are influential to the student.

Classroom Climate

Refer to Chapter 1, page 8, for more information on classroom climate.

The overall class climate is one that will either enhance or inhibit language acquisition. The classroom must be a place in which students feel respected and valued, able to take risks, and free to experiment with language.

Affective Variables

Krashen notes three "affective variables" that influence language acquisition:

- *Self-esteem:* Students with high self-esteem view themselves as capable learners and are more apt to take risks.
- *Motivation:* Motivated students are more focused and take greater risks.
- *Level of anxiety:* Anxiety inhibits language acquisition. Anxious students tend to focus on form rather than communication, and take fewer risks.[29]

STRATEGIES FOR ENGLISH LANGUAGE DEVELOPMENT

Contextualize Instruction: Create a Context for Learning

Efforts must be made to contextualize instruction or, in other words, to create a context for learning. Providing visuals or realia, previewing topics, and using anticipatory charts or guides are all examples of how to contextualize instruction in the classroom. Context greatly enhances understanding and student engagement. To illustrate this point, read the text that follows and then define *rouche.*[30]

Rouche

Favorable conditions are necessary to do this activity. That is, you have to have enough rouche. If there is too much rouche, the object might break. But if conditions are too calm, you will have problems because the rouche makes the object go up. If there are obstacles, a serious problem can result because you cannot control the rouche. Usually, rouche is most favorable during spring.

Researcher Shirley J. Adams noted that when students were asked to read this text without any comment or context, only 13% could define *rouche.* After specific background information was given, the success rate jumped to 78%. Context made the difference: *This passage is about flying a kite.*

This simple statement narrowed the range of possibilities and enabled the reader to use prior knowledge to construct meaning. Establishing context in daily instruction is ongoing. It can be simple, as in this example, or more elaborate depending on the topic and students' prior knowledge. Establishing context is, however, a powerful tool for enhancing comprehension. (For the remaining 22% who still do not understand: *rouche* means *wind.*)

TIP Promote self-confidence by celebrating all attempts at communication and praising specific appropriate behaviors.

Maintain motivation by providing instruction that is academically, linguistically, and age-level appropriate.

Promote a supportive, nurturing instructional climate. For students at earlier levels of language development, use caution in overtly correcting grammatical or other speech errors; instead, model language structures, patterns, and vocabulary to encourage even more interaction and language use. Value the fluency of ideas and comprehension over form.

Read this selection. Can you define *rouche?* Do you understand the text? (It should be pointed out that *rouche* is probably the only unfamiliar word in the entire text.) In nonfiction, often the one key content word on which comprehension hinges is unfamiliar.

How do you provide comprehensible input?

Provide Comprehensible Input

Utilize all the resources at your disposal to make instruction understandable. A list of techniques to help in providing comprehensible input is provided on page 33.

Expect Students to Learn

Maintain high expectations and a presumption of success.

Expect students to engage in English conversation and learn. Continually challenge students while supporting and expanding their approximations. Gently but insistently, require all students to engage, making it clear that each student will succeed.

Use Appropriate Questioning Strategies

Questioning strategies for English learners include using both display and referential questions and matching questions to students' levels of language proficiency.

Display and Referential Questions

Teachers tend to use two basic types of questions in the classroom:[31]

Give personal examples of each type of question.

- *Display questions:* Questions that teachers already know the answer to that simply display student knowledge or learning. *What happened first in the story? What is* 6×50?
- *Referential questions:* Questions that teachers don't know the answers to, which require students to refer to their own background knowledge or related experiences or opinions. *What was your favorite part of the story? How can you show me* 6×50?

Students will usually give us what we ask for—so *what* we ask for and *how* we ask will influence student engagement. Self-monitor your questions for one day. Which type do you most often ask? To whom? What are the contexts?

There is a place for both types of questions in the language classroom, but they are not of equivalent value. Display questions are the "traditional" teaching questions asked to check for basic comprehension and academic understandings. While they may be useful on occasion, display questions tend to limit student engagement and provide little opportunity for students to negotiate meaning or provide comprehensible output. (Note that students themselves rarely ask display questions.) Referential questions, on the other hand, are more empowering to English learners because they require students to engage themselves in language interactions at higher levels and in such a way that they understand and are understood by others. To successfully respond to referential questions, authentic thought, engagement, and language are required.

 BRAINSTORM
How can you incorporate a more referential question while ensuring comprehension?

TECHNIQUES FOR PROVIDING COMPREHENSIBLE INPUT

♦ Use visuals, realia, manipulatives, and other concrete materials.

♦ Use gestures, facial expressions, and body language.

♦ Modify your speech.

- Speak clearly, using authentic natural speech.

- Use shorter, less complex sentences for students in the earlier stages of language development.

- Maintain the natural rhythm and flow of the language.

- Speak clearly and enunciate, using authentic natural language.

♦ Use intonation, volume, and pauses to aid meaning.

♦ Contextualize ideas in relevant, real-life ways: " . . . just like you did yesterday with . . . "

♦ Repeat, rephrase, and/or paraphrase key concepts, directions, and so on.

♦ Model and demonstrate procedures and thought processes.

♦ Provide only essential information when giving directions.

♦ Build on what students already know, recognizing and extending approximations of learning and language development.

♦ Be careful of idioms and slang. Explain them when they occur.

♦ Clarify meaning in context.

♦ Encourage participation and interaction.

♦ Focus on making meaning.

♦ Maintain an environment in which students feel free to take risks.

♦ Be enthusiastic!

Refer to page 35 for sample questions for each stage.

To effectively utilize this strategy you must know students' levels of language proficiency. Refer to page 26 for an overview of these levels or stages. Observe students carefully, asking questions that match and extend their level of English.

TIP Don't rely on the question *"Do you understand?"* Students will just dutifully nod their heads and smile.

What are some of the effective strategies you have used to check comprehension? When have students fooled you?

Match Questions to Language Proficiency

All students can be encouraged to participate in discussions by varying the questions asked of individuals. Students in earlier stages of language proficiency are asked to point, gesture, or respond with words or phrases. Students with more advanced proficiency are asked questions requiring a greater amount of language in the response. *Note:* More language is *not* the same as higher-level thinking. The key is matching the question to required *speech,* not required thought. Higher-level thinking is expected of students at all levels of English language proficiency.

Check for Comprehension/Clarification

Good teachers continually monitor students' learning and comprehension. Comprehension and clarification checks should be done regularly, using a variety of techniques such as the following:

- Students restate the task.
- Students illustrate and/or describe to a partner the task and steps involved.
- Students act out or role-play directions.
- Teacher asks more "referential" questions, which require comprehension.

This ongoing interaction helps teachers monitor progress and identify areas of need or focused attention. (It may be necessary to explicitly teach students how to ask for help or clarification.)

Treat Errors and Grammar Appropriately

Speech and grammatical errors are normal and even necessary if students are to experiment with and acquire language. How to treat errors appropriately depends largely on students' level of fluency, educational background, and risk-taking behavior.[32]

In the early stages of language proficiency, fluency is much more important than accuracy. Overtly correcting errors leads to anxiety and reduces students' willingness to speak. Teachers should model appropriate language and engage students in conversations. For example, if a student says, "I goed to the park," the teacher responds, "You went to the park! What fun! What did you do?" The student benefits from hearing appropriate forms of language within the context of a real, meaningful conversation. More language is subsequently drawn from students. Focusing on correctness is reserved for times when the meaning is unclear. Again, function (meaning) takes precedence over form.

QUESTIONING TECHNIQUES FOR EACH LEVEL OF LANGUAGE PROFICIENCY

Beginning

(At this level, the questions are like commands.)

Point to the _____.

Find the _____.

Raise your hand if this is a _____.

Put the _____ on the table.

Show me the _____.

Early Intermediate

Did you enjoy the selection? Yes or no?

What color is the car?

What do I have in my hand? (one- or two-word response)

Is this hot or cold?

Are these bikes or bats?

Intermediate

How is the weather today?

Tell me about your _____.

Why? How?

What are you going to buy at the grocery store?

Early Advanced

What do you think of this text?

Compare that with your _____.

What would happen if _____?

Which do you like best? Why?

What would you do if _____?

Advanced

Grade-level appropriate questions requiring extended response.

Probably the best overall strategy is for the teacher to focus on meaning and provide communicative contexts in which students can hear, produce, and learn.

—L. Diaz-Rico and K. Weed, *The Crosscultural, Language, and Academic Development Handbook*[33]

As students progress in language proficiency, they will benefit from instruction related to systemic, or regularly occurring, errors as well as explicit instruction in the structures, patterns, and conventions of English that are essential to academic success.[34]

The effective language teacher, therefore, organizes instruction around meaningful concepts—themes, topics, areas of student interest—and deals with grammar as the need arises. This is done on an individual basis or, when the teacher notices a systemic problem among several students, [through] direct instruction. Practice on the grammar point may be directed to a small group or, when necessary, the class as a whole.

—L. Diaz-Rico and K. Weed, *The Crosscultural, Language, and Academic Development Handbook*[35]

Focus on Grammar: Ten Instructional Points

There are features of English grammar that present special challenges to English language learners. Some are eventually acquired through usage and instructive feedback, but others remain a challenge for particular students and require an explicit instructional approach. While it would probably be impossible to explicitly teach all the rules of English grammar, it makes sense to be aware of and focus on the few specific grammatical features that are routinely expected in academic settings yet typically cause confusion for students of English.

Robin Scarcella, a professor at the University of California in Irvine, works extensively with English learners enrolled in the university. Through this work she has identified ten aspects of grammar that typically present challenges to students of English. Each of these aspects, she contends, *can and should* be explicitly taught to English learners to facilitate command of academic English.[36]

COMMUNICATIVE CONTEXT

In early stages of language proficiency, fluency is more important than accuracy.

TEN INSTRUCTIONAL POINTS ON GRAMMAR

Use the following quote to help students understand nouns and verbs—particularly in their writing: "The nouns make the pictures and the verbs make those pictures move."[37]

Note the *s* rule: Find the subject and main verb. If the subject ends in an *s*, then the verb *cannot* end in an *s*. (There must be *only* one *s*.)

Nouns that remain unchanged in their plural form (*sheep*, *advice*) are noncount nouns.

The rule:
do/did + *not* + base verb = a negative sentence

Idioms and fixed expressions make no sense when taken apart. They carry meaning only as a whole.

Grammatical Features	Examples	Nonexamples
1. **Sentences** All sentences have one subject and one main verb.	My English <u>teacher</u> at school <u>was</u> the only one who helped me.	My <u>teacher</u> at school only one to help me.
2. **Subject-Verb Agreement** Subjects must agree with verbs in number (the *s* rule).	The birds fly. The bird flies.	The bird fly.
3. **Verb Tense** The present tense is used to refer to events that happen now and to indicate general truth. The past tense is used to refer to events that happened before now.	My teacher <u>explained</u> (*past tense*) to me that plants <u>need</u> (*present—general truth*) the sun.	My teacher <u>explains</u> to me that plants <u>needed</u> the sun.
4. **Verb Phrases** Some verbs are followed by *to* + base verb. Other verbs are followed by a verb ending in *-ing*.	My mom told me <u>to shut</u> the door. She encouraged <u>reading</u>.	My mom told me <u>shut</u> the door. She encouraged <u>read</u>.
5. **Plurals** A plural count noun (*book, chair*) ends in an *s*.	She likes all her <u>books</u>.	She likes all her <u>book</u>.
6. **Auxiliaries** Negative sentences are formed by placing *do/did* + *not* in front of a base verb.	Do not <u>make</u> them go.	Do not <u>makes</u> them go.
7. **Articles** Definite articles generally precede specific nouns that are modified by adjectives.	I speak <u>the</u> Spanish language. I have <u>a</u> happy heart.	I speak Spanish language. I have happy heart.
8. **Word Forms** The correct part of speech should be used—nouns for nouns, verbs for verbs, and so on.	I am completely <u>independent</u>	I am completely independence.
9. **Fixed Expressions and Idioms** Idioms and fixed expressions cannot be changed in any way. They are treated as a whole.	The cat <u>is</u> out of the bag. Hold your horses!	The cat <u>came</u> out of the bag. Hold on to your horse!
10. **Word Choice** Formal and informal words should be used in formal and informal settings or contexts, respectively.	Dear Dr. _____: (formal) Hi, Ed— (informal)	Hey, Dr. _____ (formal)

—Adapted from Scarcella, 2000.

METHODS FOR ENGLISH LANGUAGE DEVELOPMENT

How did you "learn" a foreign language? What methods were used in the classroom? How effective were they? How did you feel? What did you learn?

Both research and experience demonstrate that a second language is best learned in a manner that approximates how the first language was acquired—by using the language to meet real needs. Thus, second language programs in elementary schools should be designed on a communication-based approach—one which constantly relies on the language as the medium for the exchange of meaningful information and the communication of ideas.

—California Department of Education[38]

Using Holdaway's Model for Language Learning

Review each step of Holdaway's model. Identify how each step is incorporated in a typical language-learning activity.

Don Holdaway, in researching language acquisition, found that certain conditions related to the acquisition of spoken language were common all over the world.[39] He theorized that these conditions could serve as a model for all language learning. Following are the conditions Holdaway identified. Although not a method in the true sense, this developmental model serves to identify the conditions and instructional practices that promote language acquisition and learning in general.

- *Observation of "demonstrations":* The student observes competent adults that are admired as genuine users of language. The modeled activity is purposeful and authentic. The learner may watch, with no pressure to perform.
- *Participation:* The student is invited to participate because of a genuine need to use language (or master a particular skill). The "expert" welcomes the student while explaining, modeling, and demonstrating what to do. The act becomes collaborative.
- *Role-playing or practice:* The learner is given an opportunity to practice without observation or direction from the "expert." It is a time to self-monitor, regulate, and assess. The "expert" is nearby if needed.
- *Performance:* When the learner feels ready, he or she shares what has been accomplished and receives approval or acknowledgment.[40]

The following communication-based approaches utilize and combine many of the listed strategies to create overall approaches for English language development.

Identifying a Balanced ELD Program

Identify lessons in your ELD program that are characterized as content-, literature-, or communication-based.

What is the language focus for each? How are they the same? Different?

How do your students benefit from each?

A well-balanced English language development program provides ample opportunites to develop both conversational and academic language proficiency. The program may be structured around activities or lessons that can be characterized as follows:

- *Content-based approach:* This approach uses content as the vehicle for language development.
- *Literature-based approach:* This approach uses literature as a tool for language (including literacy) development and enrichment.

- *Communication-based approach:* This approach uses interactive activities, or language engagement, as a tool for language development. (This technique, in many instances, is similar to the *task-based approach,* which requires students to use language to accomplish a given task or solve a problem.[41])

Each of these lesson types is important for building the language competence students need for basic communicative as well as academic purposes. In addition, the areas of listening, speaking, reading, writing, and higher-order thinking skills are integrated and woven throughout. The integration of all these factors creates a balanced program leading to both communicative competence and academic success in English.

Using Total Physical Response

Total physical response (TPR) is a communicative approach that is modeled on how children acquire their first language.[42] Asher noted three basic elements:

- Listening (and understanding) precedes speaking.
- Understanding is developed through moving the body.
- Speaking is never forced.

Using TPR, the teacher gives commands while modeling the corresponding action. For example, the teacher says *"Stand up"* while standing up or *"Pick up your pencil"* while picking up a pencil. The commands are repeated and modeled until students respond easily. Gradually, the modeling aspect is removed and students respond when given only the verbal command. The process continues with increasingly more complex commands and with students taking on the role of teacher and giving commands to others.

Total Physical Response Storytelling

Blaine Ray of Bakersfield, California, expanded the notion of TPR to include storytelling. With total physical response storytelling (TPR-S), teachers model and extend language within the context of a story that students hear, see, act out, retell, and rewrite. Comprehension is enhanced as students are actively engaged in developing the language of a story that is whole and in itself supports and carries meaning. The story creates the context through which meaning is enhanced.

Teachers use the story visuals along with gestures and modeling to engage students. Students then work with partners, using the story visuals for support.

Using Content-Based ELD

This approach utilizes content, or subject-area material, as a vehicle for language acquisition and development. The content is modified to match the language proficiency of the students and is best used within a comprehensive ELD program.

Content-based ELD does not replace content area instruction. In this way, it differs from Specially Designed Academic Instruction in English (SDAIE), or Sheltered English. Content-based ELD has language acquisition as its goal, whereas SDAIE has content mastery as its goal.

Example: Using the legend of Johnny Appleseed, the teacher leads students in role-playing each action:

He places apple seeds in his pouch.
He plants the seeds.
He walks to another area.
He plants more seeds.

See Chapter 4 for more information on SDAIE.

Standards-Based English Language Development

Standards for ELD carry the additional dimension of language proficiency level. For example, a sixth grader at the early intermediate proficiency level will be working toward the sixth-grade English language arts standards. The ELD standards, however, will take into account the early language proficiency level and will provide benchmarks along the way indicating movement toward the grade-level standard.

Standards-based instruction for English language development (ELD) is similar to standards-based instruction in other subject areas: instruction is based on specific standards that provide clear expectations of what students should *know and be able to do* and also *how well* they should be able to do them.[43] ELD standards are typically linked to or may be embedded in English language arts standards. Either way, the standards provide direction and guidance to teachers in determining what students should be able to do and how well.[44]

It is this understanding that is at the heart of standards-based instruction. Teachers use the standards to develop a type of road map for focused instruction that will lead students toward attaining the grade-level standards. Teachers assess where students are now in relation to a set of given standards, and they plan instruction to support students in reaching the standards. From the beginning, assessment is built into planning and instruction and will provide evidence of student growth.

The grade-level standards reflect the expectation for *all* students.

The goal—attaining the standards—is always in mind as teachers select and utilize appropriate instructional approaches and strategies to move students toward the goal.

Gaye Burns, from San Diego City Schools, has done extensive work in standards-based ELD instruction. Page 41 provides a sample planning guide for effectively planning standards-based ELD instruction, based on her work.[45]

TOOLS FOR ENGLISH LANGUAGE AND LITERACY DEVELOPMENT

Through literature, they begin to own the new language they are hearing.

—D. Lapp, J. Flood, and J. Tinajero, *Are We Communicating?*[46]

Literature

Literature serves as a rich resource for language and literacy development. Quality literature cultivates language, provides language models, and promotes language acquisition.[47] As students listen to and participate in reading poems, rhythm and patterned books, and other rich literature, they experience language that is meaningful and contextualized. Vocabulary, patterns of speech, idioms, and concepts are developed and clarified.

TIP Utilize multicultural literature representing the backgrounds of your students. Encourage students to record the stories of their parents and grandparents to preserve their cultural heritage and use the recordings for further language and literacy development.

Refer to Chapter 3 for more on literature, text selection, and literacy and language development.

Nonfiction Texts

Life is nonfiction.

—Beverly Kobrin, in *Nonfiction Matters.*[48]

Nonfiction texts that are clear and uncluttered in terms of language and format are of particular benefit to beginning English learners. The context is clear and students bring their prior knowledge to the text. Nonfiction texts that include photographs appear more sophisticated and relevant to older students than do many works of fiction at their level.

Throughout life, the majority of reading and writing that people do is nonfiction. Nonfiction is all around us. Resources such as maps, globes, brochures (all types—travel, camp, etc.), catalogs, newspapers, magazines, and books are readily available at all levels of sophistication. All these sources of nonfiction share a common purpose: they are meant to inform. We read nonfiction to learn.[49]

STANDARDS-BASED ELD PLANNING GUIDE

English Language Arts Standard
Grade-level standard

ELD Proficiency Level(s)
- ☐ Beginning
- ☐ Early intermediate
- ☐ Intermediate
- ☐ Early advanced
- ☐ Advanced

ELD Standards (Reading, Writing, Listening, Speaking, Viewing)
Corresponding ELD standard, determined by ELD proficiency level.

Instruction/Assessment
Instruction is intertwined with assessment. Instruction must result in student attaining—or developing—the identified standard. Assessment will inform how success will be seen and measured.

Include instructional strategies.

Key Vocabulary/Language Structures/Grammar
Identify key vocabulary and language features to develop or highlight.

Materials
Identify needed materials that will both support and enhance language development.

—Adapted from Burns, 2002.

Nonfiction text is composed of language that is functional and topic specific; in other words, it is highly contextualized. When students pick up a book about fish, they immediately have a context for understanding. Nonfiction typically includes language supports students can use to enhance understanding and extend language. Features such as visuals, diagrams, headings and captions, and text organized around specific points or subpoints are of particular benefit to English learners and serve as "mini-scaffolds" to comprehension.

Nonfiction text provides abundant models of academic language in authentic contexts. Students immersed in nonfiction will be better prepared to tackle the increasingly academic requirements of grade-level work.

Music

Like literature, music serves to enrich and extend language development. Students hear language used in its most lyrical form. Evidence shows that music (and the language encoded within it) enters the brain and is processed differently from spoken language. This may account for why song lyrics are remembered for years. The pattern and flow of language within a musical context provides opportunities for students to develop language in a nonthreatening, meaningful, and fun way.

TIP Display visuals, realia, and sketches or role-play the song to help convey meaning. Students may join in with the music, but it doesn't guarantee comprehension.

Video/DVD

Carefully selected videos can serve to greatly enhance language and literacy. Videos are a natural tool for language development. They provide a medium in which students can see and hear language that is purposeful, varied, and highly contextualized. Students hear language used for a variety of purposes or functions and from many different English models. Videos provide abundant context clues from which students draw meaning. Visuals, gestures, auditory clues, actions, and interactions within a purposeful whole all contribute to providing one of the basic tenets of language acquisition—messages that are understandable.

Videos (or DVDs) can be incorporated into varied teaching strategies. Refer to Chapter 3, page 74, for information on using videos for a "directed-viewing" activity.

Additionally, videos are highly motivating yet nonthreatening. Students usually engage in viewing videos in a comfortable, low-anxiety environment.

Clearly, not all videos are appropriate or valuable for the classroom. Those used must be carefully and critically selected. A suitable video should be:

- *Complete:* Presenting a whole story, idea, or process, not fragmented pieces of visual or auditory images
- *Relevant:* Compatible with student interests, age, and level of language proficiency
- *Engaging:* Based on an authentic work of literature or a documentary that engages students over time with repeated viewings
- *Brief:* Able to capture and hold attention without overburdening students with complex story structure or vocabulary

To achieve the greatest benefit from viewing a video, students must be active participants. *Active viewing* is accomplished by structuring lessons and utilizing strategies that create a context and purpose for viewing the video and encourage high levels of student interaction.

CD-ROM/Computer Technology

CD-ROM and other computer technologies are increasingly important tools for language and literacy development. Increasing numbers of software programs, games, and activities effectively present information that is contextualized and highly visual, with ample spoken and written language cues. "Voiced" programs now sound quite human, and authentic interaction and meaningful language activities are now available. Programs can be modified and structured to match the specific needs of students. Programs that allow students to "read along" or explore by "pointing and clicking" are effective in developing language and literacy. Simple word-processing programs that provide support for language conventions, including spelling and grammar, also are useful tools for developing students' written English skills. As with any instructional resources, computer software must be purposeful, age-appropriate, engaging, and of specific value to the students for whom it is selected.

Identify the CD-ROM or other computer programs you have found useful for developing English.

Visuals, Manipulatives, and Realia

An abundance of resources that can be used to contextualize language, making it visible and tangible, are invaluable tools for the language classroom. Select print materials that are rich in visuals and color. Supplement with magazines, newspapers, or calendar pictures (start a picture file), maps, charts, and models. Provide materials and hands-on activities that will enable students use all their senses to develop conceptual understanding. Use videos, the overhead projector, the chalkboard, filmstrips, props, and other real objects.

What visuals, manipulatives, and realia do you have immediate access to? How can you incorporate these resources in daily instruction?

 BRAINSTORM
What additional resources do you need to create a language-rich classroom?

REVIEW

Refer to and review the Preview page for this chapter (page 17). Was your prior knowledge accurate? (Did you have any misconceptions or inaccurate ideas?)

What did you LEARN about language and language acquisition?

How can you apply this information? (Include one or two specific ideas.)

What else do you want to know?

CHAPTER 3

Literacy Development

> I believe in the power of language. It is through this power, both spoken and written, that we preserve our principles, practices, and institutions as a democracy. For our students, literacy is a key to academic success, higher education, career development, citizenship, and personal enrichment. If we wish to provide all students an equal opportunity to learn, it is essential that we do whatever it takes to ensure success in literacy for every student.
>
> —Delaine Easton, in California Department of Education[1]

Read the following text and then answer the questions in complete sentences.

A krinklejup was parling a tristlebin. A barjam stipped. The barjam grupped "Minto" to the krinklejup. The krinklejup zisked zoely.

1. What was the krinklejup doing?
2. What stipped?
3. What did the barjam grup?
4. How did the krinklejup zisk?[2]

Is this reading? Some might argue that this is reading—we can speak the words and answer the questions. This is what many English learners do. They appear to be doing well; they "read" beautifully and answer the questions correctly, yet they still have difficulty in many types of literacy activities.

An English learner, in his fourth year in a U.S. school—and a fluent reader—was asked the same question: Is this reading? His perceptive response:

"Yes, because I could work out the answers." Then he added, "But it's not really reading, because I just went from here," indicating the questions, "to here," indicating the text. "It didn't go through my head."[3]

Reading is reading only when *it goes through your head*—when meaning is drawn from print. Reading is about making meaning. This is true for all students. Students who are learning the English language in all its domains—listening, speaking, reading, and writing—have more meaning to make.

What do you already KNOW about literacy development?

What do you WANT to know or learn?

Could you answer the questions on page 46? (If you answered "yes," you're a good reader. Literacy skills transfer across languages.

Did you understand the excerpt?

Were you reading?

CUEING SYSTEMS

Research affirms that English learners in particular benefit most from a *top-down* approach to literacy. The top-down approach moves from the whole to the parts and back to the whole again, recognizing that background knowledge, experience, and understanding play an important role in making meaning. Goodman[4] suggests that good readers interact with text through a series of predictions, verifications, rejections, and more predictions. Students integrate what they know about the world with the coordinated application of three major cueing systems to construct meaning from text.[5]

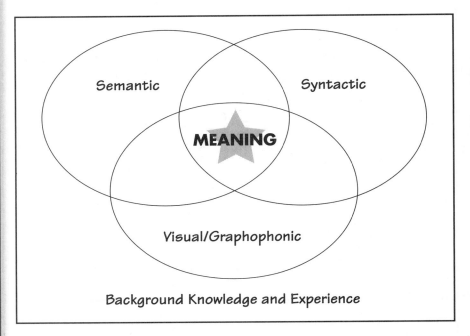

Background Knowledge and Experience

Semantic: This system focuses on meaning—what is happening. *Does it make sense?*

Syntactic: This system utilizes knowledge of language patterns and grammatical structures. *Does it sound right?*

Visual/Graphophonic: This system focuses on sound/symbol relationships and visual aspects of language. *Does it look right?*

Background knowledge: Although background knowledge is not a cueing system in the strictest sense, it forms the foundation for the other three cueing systems and how they are utilized.

Clearly, all three cueing systems, combined with background knowledge, work together in creating meaning from print. Good readers tend to be flexible, using and integrating the systems interdependently. Developing readers, however, may rely too heavily on one system, typically graphophonic cues.[6] Each system, used in isolation, presents special challenges for English learners.

Semantic meaning is largely based on shared background and cultural or linguistic knowledge. English learners tend to have gaps in these areas.

Syntactic meaning is based on internalized grammar and linguistic structures. English learners may not yet have internalized the structures needed to access this system.

Visual/Graphophonic meaning comes largely from understanding the verbal connection to written symbols. English contains more meaningful sounds than most other prominent languages. Many English learners first have to learn to "hear" the sound before they can produce it based on a printed symbol.

English learners in particular benefit from a balanced literacy program, one in which background knowledge and *all three* cueing systems are utilized and fully developed.

DEVELOPING STRATEGIC READERS

Instructional strategies become reading strategies when a student can independently select an appropriate one and use it effectively to construct meaning from a text.

—California Department of Education[7]

Reading includes both decoding and making meaning, but meaning is at the heart of reading. Reading, therefore, is an active process in which students think, reason, and apply strategies to construct meaning. When asked the question *What is reading?* a student responded:

Reading is thinking . . . when you read, you have to figure out the words and what they mean. Sometimes it's easy. Sometimes it's hard.[8]

To help students become good readers, it is necessary to understand what good readers do. There is a growing body of research that consistently indicates that competent readers use a range of strategies more effectively and with greater flexibility than do less proficient readers.[9] The following summarizes what active, engaged, and thoughtful readers do to construct meaning as they read. Proficient readers:

- Have a running dialog with (or talk back to) the text, asking questions of themselves, the author, and the text itself.
- Visualize scenes and characters, creating images using different senses.
- Draw inferences during and after reading and make predictions.
- Relate prior knowledge to reading and search for connections between what is known and what is being read.
- Synthesize information within and between texts and readings.
- Read with a specific purpose and distinguish important from less important ideas in the text.
- Monitor comprehension and apply "fix-up" strategies when needed.
- Accept ambiguity and push on; when unsure of the meaning of a portion of text, keep reading, confident that the meaning will become clear.

Strategy instruction for English learners should always begin with what students know and are able to do. This context is used as the basis for extending and expanding language and learning.

These key strategies must be learned and applied: *Students must be explicitly taught how to use the strategies effectively.* Further, instruction must be organized in such a way that there is an *expectation* that students will learn to apply these strategies on their own; as students progress in their learning, *instruction gradually shifts from teacher-directed to student-directed.*

GRADUAL RELEASE OF RESPONSIBILITY: *TO, WITH, BY*

Effective literacy instruction includes explicit teaching in the strategies students are expected to acquire. The instructional approaches used for a given strategy gradually evolve from teacher controlled and directed to student controlled and self-directed. This gradual release of responsibility is consistent with key research regarding how students learn.[10] (Also refer to Cambourne's conditions for learning[11] in the next section.)

An effective literacy program will provide a variety of approaches that together support the gradual release of responsibility as illustrated in the diagrams that follow.

- *Initially, instruction is provided **to** students.* Students engage in new learning that is largely controlled by the teacher. The students actively listen, discuss, and join in as directed by the teacher.
- *Responsibility for learning is shared **with** students.* Students share control with teachers as they begin to take on new learning with direct support and coaching from the teacher.
- *Finally, responsibility is assumed **by** students.* Students reach independence and are in full control of the process with little or no teacher support.

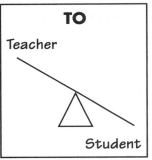

TO
Teacher
Student

Teacher maintains the greater control, explaining, modeling, and demonstrating new strategies and skills. Students actively participate through listening and talk (conversation).

Instructional approaches:
Read aloud, modeled writing

WITH
Teacher   Student

Teachers and students share responsibility for learning as instruction continues. Teachers coach and engage students, providing ongoing support and feedback. Students begin to take on learning through approximations and practice.

Instructional approaches:
Shared reading, guided reading, language experience, shared writing, interactive writing

You must continually assess student need:
- *What does the student need at this time to move him or her to the next level?*
- *What strategies is the student applying consistently, inconsistently, not at all?*
- *Which strategy is the most critical for the student now?*

You must then match instructional approaches and/or strategies work to the assessed need:
- *How will I get the student there?*
- *Which strategy or skill does the student need now?*
- *Which instructional approach will most effectively support the learning?*

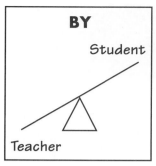

Students assume primary responsibility for their learning and independently apply the strategy/learning to new situations. Teachers build on this strength to move students to higher levels of learning (again utilizing **to** and **with** strategies for new learning).

Instructional approaches:

Independent reading and writing

Instruction within this model is fluid. As students move to independence in specific tasks (at the **by** level), the teacher is already working on other, higher-level tasks that require greater instructional support at the **to** and **with** levels. There will be times when specific groups of students require several days of support utilizing **to** and **with** strategies. Other students may need only minimal support in a specific area before they are off and running. The key is to know the learners, provide the level of support needed, and sustain the level of support until students reach independence. This instructional practice is very different from the "tell and test" method of teaching in which a teacher presents a lesson, permits independent practice, and then tests students, often wondering why the students haven't learned.

The **to, with, by** structure provides the challenges with support and the expectation of success that English learners need to reach high levels of literacy and academic learning in their new language.

This instructional practice is often compared to a dance, in which teachers glide between approaches in response to student moves and actions. Students are at the center of learning and teachers respond with supports as student needs dictate.

CONDITIONS FOR LEARNING

Brian Cambourne observed and documented hundreds of students as they were engaged in acquiring literacy.[12] He used this information to identify and develop conditions that promote student engagement and result in high levels of language acquisition and learning in general. These conditions for learning provide an insightful overview of instructional practices that directly affect student learning and language acquisition. They suggest activities for reflection: immersion, demonstration, expectation, responsibility, employment, approximations, and response.

Balanced Literacy

Balanced literacy is the principled application of a number of instructional approaches and strategies that bring balance to the task of learning to read. The strategies are grounded in beliefs and understandings about how language—and specifically literacy—is acquired and developed. A balanced approach to literacy combines rich language and literacy experiences with explicit literacy instruction in decoding and encoding.[13] This strategic integration of a range of approaches and strategies provides students with the skills and knowledge necessary to be proficient readers, writers, and users of language.

Refer to page 52 for tips on using Cambourne's conditions for learning.

Outline ways in which you have used each of Cambourne's conditions in developing students' language ability and literacy.

CAMBOURNE'S CONDITIONS FOR LEARNING
WITH CLASSROOM APPLICATIONS

IMMERSION: Students are surrounded with print.
The classroom is "dripping with print." Environmental print is affixed to walls, doors, and furniture. A comfortable, orderly classroom library invites students to select books. Authentic reading and writing are in evidence everywhere!

DEMONSTRATION: Students learn through modeling.
Teachers and students model listening, speaking, reading, and writing throughout the day. Teachers model reading a variety of texts or writing using an overhead projector. Students observe literacy used daily in a variety of ways.

EXPECTATION: Students are expected to learn and work at increasingly complex, appropriate tasks.
The classroom is well-supplied with age-appropriate materials. Students have materials that match their independent and instructional literacy levels. The classroom is structured with the expectation of learning and academic success.

RESPONSIBILITY: Students share responsibility for their learning.
The classroom is student-centered and structured so that students take increasing responsibility for their learning including classroom procedures, cleanliness and orderliness, completion of tasks, and obtaining resources and information. The teacher serves as an informed facilitator, resource, and guide.

EMPLOYMENT: Students are actively engaged in purposeful learning.
Students are engaged in meaningful activities that promote a feeling of ownership. They participate in authentic literacy activities such as reading and writing conferences with the teacher and/or peers, process writing, and publishing works. Materials and human resources are utilized to serve this purpose.

APPROXIMATIONS: Students take risks, feel free to experiment, and are celebrated for their efforts.
Instruction and learning is structured so that all students learn and can succeed. Risk-taking behavior is rewarded. Approximations to the standard are recognized and celebrated. Students' work is displayed and celebrated.

RESPONSE: Students receive positive and specific feedback.
Activities such as author's chair, conferencing, self-evaluation, and cooperative and collaborative learning provide opportunities for feedback from peers and teachers. This feedback is, in most cases, immediate, specific, and constructive.

Adapted from *The Whole Story: Natural Learning and the Acquisition of Literacy in the Classroom* by Brian Cambourne, © 1988, by permission of Scholastic New Zealand Limited.

A fundamental idea of balanced literacy is that reading and writing are best learned by reading and writing. Students must be engaged in meaningful literacy experiences and enterprises. Through this active engagement, students develop both the personal strategies and the skills that enable them to utilize all cueing systems to draw meaning from increasingly more complex texts.

Balanced literacy promotes a range of approaches and techniques that are strategically applied and integrated to support the specific needs of students as they develop literacy. Teachers must be skilled in utilizing a variety of approaches and techniques that will guide students along the path of literacy.

PROMISING PRACTICES FOR DEVELOPING ENGLISH LITERACY

The best approach in the instruction of all novice readers and writers is to create a rich environment, steeped in authentic language and stimulating stories that vitally connect with what the [students] already know and are curious about.

—California Department of Education[14]

The literacy approaches and strategies that follow reflect current research regarding the elements of quality literacy instruction for all students. Each provides a level of teacher support and student engagement that together will move students to higher levels of literacy and academic achievement.

The approaches and strategies were selected for inclusion in this book because they are particularly effective for teaching English learners. The approaches take into account the complex relationship between literacy development and oral language development and capitalize on the relationship to push both. Better language users become better readers and writers. Similarly, active and engaged readers and writers refine and extend language proficiency. The approaches provide opportunities for literacy experiences that are bathed in authentic language through talk: discussion, conversation, questioning, reflection, and engagement at all levels.

Further, these approaches empower English learners by making them increasingly accountable for their own learning. They build on students' strengths and on the students' wealth of experience, knowledge, insight, and resources that can be drawn upon to generate additional knowledge and understanding.

The approaches share a common underlying principle: language and literacy are about understanding, and meaning is central to this enterprise. Each approach contributes to this purpose, and together they provide a solid framework for building proficiency in the English language and English literacy.

This chapter describes how to use a variety of strategies for developing each cueing system.

After reviewing the strategies, identify the ones you feel are of particular benefit for each cueing system.

Read Aloud

Read aloud introduces students to the pleasures of reading. As students are immersed in a variety of carefully chosen texts, they develop a love of reading while learning about written language. Within the context of the text, teachers model reading strategies that often exceed students' current level of competence. Read aloud is a highly supportive activity that brings about significant communicative and academic rewards:

- Development of vocabulary, language structures and patterns, and a sense of story
- Exposure to varied styles and registers of English
- Exposure to varied story and text structures, genres, authors, and language patterns and features
- Awareness of the connection between the written and spoken word and the distinct differences
- Knowledge of a variety of known texts that can be used as the basis of subsequent reading and writing activities
- Membership in a community of learners/readers who share knowledge and enjoyment
- Love of reading
- Significant opportunities for authentic talk

Through read aloud, the teacher demonstrates fluent reading with a variety of carefully selected literature that represents our diverse society. Students are able to experience texts that they are not yet able to read on their own. The teacher reads aloud to the whole class or a small group of students with similar needs. Favorite texts or parts of a text may be reread for specific instructional purposes, and students can engage in authentic conversations about the text and their connections to it.

A well-delivered read aloud allows English learners to hear text as it was meant to be read. The teacher models the rhythm and flow of English text. Fluent readings assist students in internalizing English language patterns, structures, vocabulary, stress, and intonation—all of which carry meaning in English.

Consider the difference in meaning between the following two sentences when stress is placed on different words:

- *This* is my life.
- This is *my* life.

Reading texts aloud allows opportunities to investigate these subtle yet significant carriers of meaning in text.

Shared Reading

Shared reading provides a valuable forum in which teachers model and demonstrate the reading processes and strategies needed to read fluently. Each student, regardless of reading level, can be engaged in the process of

---

Read aloud provides the firsthand experiences that teach students how print works and serves to nurture a growing awareness and understanding of print (directionality, print encoding language, formatting of print, and the fact that words are made up of letters).[15]

TIP Early readers are supported by reading selections with a strong sense of story. The story line itself—or sense of story—provides support as students negotiate new or unfamiliar language or ideas. Include selections that reflect the linguistic and cultural background of your students.

reading. Using an enlarged copy of the text or a text everyone can see (e.g., by employing an overhead projector) gives all students the opportunity to participate. Teachers and students share the task of reading a text that might otherwise be too difficult for students. Teachers provide the safe environment, constant support, and meaningful demonstrations that stretch students beyond their independent abilities.

Through shared reading, teachers introduce, identify, discuss, and help students interpret the many conventions, structures, and features of written texts such as illustrations, diagrams and charts, punctuation, captions, and specific text structures. Teachers can also use the shared experience to extend and amplify oral language or compare and contrast the frequent differences between "book language" and "spoken language" and point out important language patterns.

Through shared reading, students share in the enjoyment of reading and actively participate as they listen, discuss, and read along with the teacher.[16] Shared reading offers great flexibility for the teacher in customizing the experience to match student needs.

- A shared reading experience can include the whole class or a small group with specific needs.

- Teachers can read new texts or revisit familiar texts. Students bring an understanding of the general language, content, and structure of familiar texts and can focus their attention on the strategy being taught.[17] Rereading a text also supports students in increasing language and reading fluency.

Step by Step: Shared Reading

1. *Identify the purpose or focus of the reading.* Determine the strategy or skill that students need. (For early readers or those new to English, it could be listening to and participating in fluent English reading.)

2. *Select the text.* Select high-interest, age-appropriate texts that support the purpose of the reading and that can be comfortably completed in one sitting. The text can be above the students' independent reading level because the teacher will provide needed support. Look for texts that provide language clues, context, and supports and are "considerate" of students' increasing English proficiency.

3. *Read the selection to students.* Model fluent reading and language use, using natural intonation and expression. Emphasize the dramatic qualities of the text. Read straight through, pausing only for important predictions or comments. Engage students in talk about the text.

4. *Reread the selection.* Read the selection again, helping students become familiar with its content and structure. Students may actively participate through discussion, reading portions with the teacher, "echo" reading, adding actions, or adding sound.

5. *Revisit familiar texts.* Use the selection to focus on a specific strategy or skill that students need. Model and demonstrate how good readers apply the strategy or skill. Encourage students to identify, practice, and apply the strategy or skill using the familiar text.

Younger students and those new to English are supported by texts that are predictable and/or contain rhythm and rhyme. However, avoid nonsense stories as students will try to make sense of nonsense. For older students, select a short story, chapter, or excerpt from a text that incorporates good examples of the strategies or skills that will be modeled and practiced.

Patricia Cunningham identifies three criteria for selecting shared reading books for younger students:[18]
1. Predictability
2. Appeal
3. Ability to "take us someplace" conceptually

For older students, similar criteria should be considered:
1. Appeal and age appropriateness
2. Ability to take us someplace conceptually
3. Emotional connection
4. Examples of the strategies and skills students are learning

Refer to pages 60 and 64 for more on text selection.

TIP Creating innovations of poetry and rhyming or patterned stories provides good opportunities for developing phonics and phonemic awareness.

6. *Extend the learning (optional)*. Students may write about a text, read it again to partners, read it again independently, or engage in additional work or activities to extend understanding, language, or vocabulary and/or further develop specific strategies or skills. For example, students might make story re-creations or innovations, plays, research projects, or comparison charts or grids. (*Note:* Be sure that the time spent on extended activities is time well spent.)

Think Aloud

Both shared reading and read aloud lend themselves to using a think-aloud strategy to promote greater student comprehension. During the reading of the text, the teacher will pause and ponder out loud aspects of the text or specific reading strategies that are being used. For example:

- *That didn't make sense to me, so I am going to go back and reread that paragraph.*
- *I wonder why she isn't going to tell her mother what happened. Why would she keep it a secret? I bet she thinks her mom won't believe her because she lied before.*

With think alouds, teachers model their thinking and give students concrete examples of how to use specific reading strategies to construct meaning.[19]

Guided Reading

Guided reading is a teaching approach designed to help individual students learn how to process increasingly challenging texts with understanding and fluency.

—Irene C. Fountas and Gay Su Pinnell, *Guiding Readers and Writers, Grades 3–6*[20]

TIP Guided reading provides many opportunities to develop and refine language.

Guided reading provides opportunities for students to practice and apply the reading strategies they have learned and are learning, thereby taking on greater responsibility for their reading. As students read, they are guided by the teacher, who nudges, prompts, and coaches them through the text, often referring to strategies that have been introduced and modeled in shared reading or read aloud. The purpose is to help students recognize the resources in themselves and in the text that will enable them to overcome difficulties in the text.[21] The teacher works with a small group of students with similar instructional needs at a particular point in time. The groups are dynamic—that is, continually reshaped to meet divergent student needs.[22]

Text selection is a critical factor in guided reading. Texts should meet the following criteria:

Leveled books: Having a wealth of books and other pieces of text at reading levels that match your students' instructional level is critical to successful guided reading.

- Match the *instructional* level of the student group—be slightly above their independent reading level. The text allows students to apply what they already know and extends this processing power with a few new challenges that students will be able to overcome with the guidance and prompting of the teacher.
- Support the strategies and skills students are practicing.
- Carry sufficient supports as well as appropriate challenges to help students read at increasingly higher levels.

- Be considerate in terms of language supports and challenges: containing largely familiar vocabulary and language patterns while providing adequate supports and contexts for new or more challenging language patterns and structures.

One of the most significant features of guided reading is the sharing of responsibility between teacher and student. Students are expected to take responsibility for their learning and apply what they know. They are able to do more with help than they can do independently—and soon take this learning to independence. The guided reading experience encourages students to develop reading skills and strategies at increasingly higher levels, and promotes student confidence and their belief in themselves as readers.

The small-group format of guided reading provides an excellent forum for students to talk and negotiate meaning. *There is power in the group.* Teachers can facilitate and shape the talk to clarify thinking and further support students with expanded vocabulary and language structures (through questioning and modeling), thus enabling students to give words to thought.

Step by Step: Guided Reading

Successful implementation of guided reading depends on selecting appropriate instructional texts day after day.

—Irene C. Fountas and Gay Su Pinnell, *Matching Books to Readers*[23]

1. *Form the small group.* Maintain accurate observation and conferring notes for all students. Review the notes and look for trends. Based on this information, group students with similar instructional needs and determine the immediate instructional focus for each group.

2. *Select the text.* Carefully select the text to support the instructional focus and meet student needs. Every student in the group needs a copy of the text. Every student in the group will read part or all of the text during the guided reading lesson.

3. *Draw students to the selection.* Provide a "rich introduction" to the text, discussing the title, cover, and illustrations or pictures. Guide students in creating a context for the text. Encourage predictions and tap into background knowledge and related experiences. Challenge students to make connections to the text and draw on prior knowledge to support their thinking.

4. *Picture walk and talk (appropriate for texts with pictures or visuals).* Talk students through the book. Engage students in talk as they describe the illustrations, create context, and note details to assist in constructing meaning. *Intentionally use and discuss the unfamiliar vocabulary and language structures students will encounter in the text.* Encourage students to engage in conversation with each other concerning the text.

5. *Have students read the text.* Each student reads the text independently. Interact briefly with each student, monitoring reading and prompting students to apply strategies as needed. (As a variation, students may also read with partners.)

TIP Observe students carefully. Use this opportunity to refine and extend language. Note the range and depth of language students are using. Use this information to inform instruction.

6. *Discuss and revisit the text.* Discuss the text as a group, encouraging all students to engage, discuss, and comment on the meaning of the text as well as their use of strategies and skills. This talk encourages students to co-construct meaning, clarify thinking, and develop the functional language necessary to engage in discourse.

7. *Extending the meaning of the text (optional).* Students may write about the text, analyze aspects of the text, read it again to partners, read again independently, or engage in additional work or activities to extend understanding, language, or vocabulary and/or further develop specific strategies or skills. (*Note:* Plan carefully to ensure that time spent on extended activities is time well spent.)

Independent Reading

Surveys conducted as part of the National Assessment of Educational Progress suggest the simplest of all solutions (for fostering improved reading): Encourage and challenge students to read.

—Education Week[24]

"Independent reading is not a stage to be reached but a part of every stage of reading." (Margaret Mooney[26])

Numerous research studies demonstrate that there is a significant relationship between volume of reading and reading achievement.[25] Independent reading is the principal means by which students are encouraged to read huge quantities of interesting and accessible books. Independent reading encompasses reading for a variety of purposes and gives students opportunities to practice the strategies they have been developing through other literacy activities.[27]

Classrooms must contain a range of books that students have access to and that they can read on their own.

Teachers assist students in learning how to select appropriate texts—that is, texts at their independent reading level. For independent reading, students must have access to a great number of books that match their independent reading level. These are texts that students can read on their own and that possess few reading challenges. Students should be able to read these books with a high degree of accuracy and fluency.

Independent reading is also a component of reading workshop. Learning is strongly supported when independent reading is accompanied by conferring.

Individual Student Conference: Conferring

Conferring . . . first involves research in order to learn where the child is as a reader and understand the child's intention, then deciding what we should teach, and then teaching in a way that can influence what that child does on another day with another book.

—Lucy McCormick Calkins, *The Art of Teaching Reading*[28]

Conferring involves one-on-one conferences with students that are designed to gather information about each student as a reader and to provide a forum for direct, explicit, and targeted support. The teacher can identify specific needs, provide expert guidance and instruction, and direct and refocus students. Lucy McCormick Calkins[29] identifies three elements of conferring:

1. *Research:* Observe students in various literacy contexts. Note trends or significant occurrences. During conferring, question to gather more information about students as readers and their utilization of reading strategies.

2. *Decide:* Decide what students need now. What is the next step?

3. *Teach:* Draw students' attention to what you observed and decided. Point out strategies and skills students should continue to work on or begin to apply. With the student, decide on a focus and follow up in subsequent meetings.

Maintain accurate records of what happened during each conference. Include observations and note the strategy(ies) the student should work on. Conference notes are invaluable for keeping track of individual readers and their reading behaviors: what is or is not being applied to their reading; what was discussed; what strategies the student will work on.

Sample Questions to Guide a Reading Conference

- To begin the conference, focus the student on reader self-awareness:
  What are you working on now in reading?
  Where do you see yourself as a reader?
  How is your reading going?

- Focus the student on learning and strategy application:
  What strategies do you find you use?
  What seems hard for you?
  Tell me about your text choice? (Why did you choose this book?)
  How are you handling confusing parts or tricky words?
  Did you reread any parts? Tell me why.
  How is this helping you grow as a reader?
  Can you read this part to me?

- Relate strategy to mini-lesson:
  Show me how/where you tried (the strategy from today's lesson).
  How are you using _____ in your reading?

Reading Workshop

The workshop model organizes instruction and supports students in their learning. Students are engaged in daily reading and interactions with others about the reading. Reading workshop replicates what "real readers" do: read, reflect, discuss, and respond. The process and procedures are tailored to students' needs and interests.[30] Teachers begin with a mini-lesson—brief, direct instruction in a short lesson that focuses on a specific literacy strategy or skill. Students then practice the strategy or skill independently or with partners (independent practice). Teachers check in with students, monitoring and providing guidance and feedback (conferring). Finally, students have a chance to debrief with the whole group to discuss their own application of the reading strategy from the mini-lesson.

Step by Step: Reading Workshop

1. *Mini-lesson*

   - Determine the instructional focus. Identify a specific strategy or skill that students need.
   - Read aloud or shared reading? Determine which approach best supports the modeling and demonstration of the focus strategy or skill.
   - Present the mini-lesson using the selected text and approach. Engage students in conversation about the strategy.

TIP For easy reference, keep your conference notes in a three-ring binder with a tabbed divider for each student. Jot down notes when conferring. Refer to the notes to ensure coherent support and guidance.

TIP Plan and prepare for the reading workshop by asking yourself questions:

- *How does the focus of the mini-lesson support students in becoming better readers?*
- *What is my expectation for learning? What will the students be able to do at the end of this workshop?*
- *If asked, what will the students say they are learning?*
- *What text should I use? What texts should students use?*
- *Whom should I confer with today?*

Prepare English learners for the "share" part of the workshop: *I am going to ask you to share this when we have our share time. Let's practice what you will say.* Assist students with the language needed to convey their thoughts. Casually ask the students to share with the group. Encourage talk and analysis with questions:

- *Who else used the strategy this way?*
- *Who did something like this?*
- *Did you make a connection with what _____ did?*

- Restate the focus and direct students to practice the focus strategy or skill as they read independently: "Today when you're reading, I want you to _____."

2. *Independent practice/reading with conferring*
   - Students independently practice the mini-lesson strategy or skill using books at their independent reading level.
   - While students are reading, confer with individuals to monitor strategic reading, provide feedback, and direct students to the next steps. Also, identify students who are demonstrating an understanding and application of the mini-lesson and can bring something significant to share in the follow-up.

3. *Share or follow-up*
   - Restate the focus of the mini-lesson. Ask individuals you observed to share new understandings or applications of the mini-lesson, leading all students to engage in a conversation about their reading.
   - Determine next steps: Depending on student performance, determine whether the instructional focus should be continued with more modeling and demonstration or should move on to a new strategy or skill.

Text Analysis and Selection

Text Analysis

Refer to the Analyzing Text form on page 63.

Text analysis involves the careful examination of a text in order to identify the specific elements that will support and/or challenge students in their reading. Examining a text from the perspective of the student—in particular a student who is still learning English—helps teachers develop a deeper understanding of what students must do to process text. The subtleties and nuances of a text that often obscure meaning become visible, and teachable.

Analyzing text promotes a deeper awareness of how a text works—how it hangs together and is constructed. Text supports and challenges become apparent, and teachers can more skillfully select texts that match student needs and then deliver instruction that enables students to reveal and construct meaning at increasingly higher levels.

The process requires reading the book (or the text) and then analyzing it in different ways, from differing perspectives, to identify and understand the supports and challenges in the text. Teachers then make determinations about the appropriateness of the text—for a specific purpose for specific students. For example, texts selected for independent reading should contain few challenges. However, texts selected for the purpose of modeling a specific strategy or skill through read aloud or shared reading should stretch students to the next level with challenges that can be supported and scaffolded by the teacher.

Key characteristics for text analysis include the following:

Genre: Category of fiction or nonfiction texts with similar characteristics (fantasy, historical fiction, biography, informational text).

Structure: The way a text is presented. Narratives, both fiction and nonfiction, are usually given in a story format. Expository texts are usually nonfiction texts that use text structures (for example, cause-effect, chronological order) to organize information and aid coherence. Textbooks are typically expository texts.

Familiarity with how a given genre works promotes understanding.

Understanding and recognizing a text's structure helps English learners retain meaning as they navigate through text.

Content/Themes/Ideas: What the text is about. The content, theme, or ideas of a text may be familiar or unfamiliar to students and therefore represent a support or a challenge.

Strategies for making meaning: Strategies students learn and apply to enhance understanding. Texts frequently lend themselves to supporting specific strategies such as inferring, making connections, or visualizing. Texts also lend themselves to specific instructional approaches such as shared reading or read aloud.

Levels of comprehension: The layers of comprehension that are embedded in a text. Students must understand a text and the author's intent on many levels:

- *Literal:* Meaning is explicitly stated in the text. *What is the boy's name?*

- *Inferential:* Meaning is not explicit but implied in the text. *Why did he shake his head and smile?*

- *Applied:* Meaning must be constructed outside the text by the reader. *Why would someone do this? Why do you think the author wrote this story?*

Prior knowledge: The internal resources students bring to a text. Tapping into what students know about language and language use, culture, and related life experiences creates a context for meaning. This knowledge, in English or the home language, serves as a building block to further learning. Prior knowledge is a support, but not an essential requirement to learning or understanding. Otherwise, we could learn only what we already know! Students must be flexible in learning and reading and develop the capacity to tackle and comprehend completely unfamiliar topics and texts. We must help students recognize and develop their own flexibility so that they better comprehend more challenging "context-reduced" content.

Literary features/devices: Stylistic devices that are inserted in or woven throughout text. Readers are expected to make meaning by recognizing and properly interpreting a variety of literary features such as point of view, dialog, and chronology (for example, simple narratives, flashbacks, and stories within stories). Literary features significantly affect the readability of a text.

Language features/devices: Text features that represent language use at the word, sentence, or whole-text level. Idioms, rhythm and rhyme, figurative language, metaphors and similes, dialect, and active/passive voice are all examples of language devices used in a text. Vocabulary and word use profoundly influence understanding. Vocabulary development must include instruction and practice in words that can be thought of as *brick* (content and concepts) and *mortar* (conjunctions, prepositions, and other "utility" words). To form complete and cohesive sentences, the more tangible "brick" words are held together with the more elusive "mortar" words. Language complexity—the syntactical patterns and grammatical structures embedded in a text—can range from simple and straightforward to extremely complex and convoluted.

TIP Focus on strategies that will have the biggest payoff for your students now. Which will best support understanding?

English learners must be supported with the language to comprehend and express their understanding on all three levels.

TIP Prompt and gently push student to the higher levels of comprehension.

TIP Tap into students' prior knowledge and make explicit connections between what they already know and are learning.

TIP Provide experiences with varied texts. Model and point out how literary features influence meaning, and chart the language that often signals the device.

By their nature, language devices often present particular challenges to English learners. Engaging in meaningful text is, however, a principal tool for language and vocabulary development. Refer to page 70 for a list of signal (or mortar) words.

Refer to page 71 for a description of cohesive devices.

Plan for talk. Identify parts of text that lend themselves to talk. Model literary talk: asking questions, wondering, and using vocabulary in context.

Refer to Gibbons's "Selecting Text for English Learners" on page 64.

Language cohesion: Cohesive devices are used to connect and hold language together to provide coherent, fluent speech and text. Five specific cohesive devices—reference, substitution, ellipses, conjunctions, and lexical cohesion—are described in detail later in this chapter.

Engagement: Opportunities to talk and reflect. Talk profoundly influences thought. Through talk we clarify, question, inspire, and negotiate meaning. English learners need constant opportunities for rich and authentic conversation with individuals, partners, small groups, and the whole class. As students engage in purposeful talk, they co-construct meaning and practice using more academic forms of language.

Book/Print features: Features related to the physical aspects of the text. The actual look of a text can be supportive—or "considerate"—or it can pose challenges—that is, be "inconsiderate." Book or print features include text length and organization (chapters, headings, logical breaks, and so on), font, spacing, size, page layout, and visuals (illustrations, photographs, charts, diagrams, and so on).

Analyzing a text promotes a deeper awareness of how a text works—how it hangs together and is constructed. One can more readily see into the text and identify potential supports, challenges, and teaching opportunities. Text analysis results in teachers who select appropriate texts and skillfully lead students to use the text and their own internal resources to construct meaning.

The Analyzing Text form on the facing page identifies key characteristics for analyzing text. This form can be used to scrutinize texts carefully and identify text characteristics that are potentially supportive and/or challenging to English learners.

Text Selection

In general, text selection is affected by a number of key factors including student age and interests, student reading level, purpose for reading, and suitability for the selected approach or strategy. Pauline Gibbons provides further thoughts on selecting texts that are supportive to English learners who are learning to read in a new language.[31] Gibbons's ideas about selecting fiction and nonfiction texts are described in a concise format on page 64.

Teachers must weigh the potential value of a text (for example, good use of specific features or devices students must learn) against its challenges to determine its suitability for particular students at a particular time. In other words, to make good choices about text, teachers must know their students and they must know the text.

Features that are particularly supportive of English learners include clear and consistent text markings and layout, a clear font, and visuals that enhance understanding of the text.

ANALYZING TEXT

Title, Author, (Level)	
Genre	
Structure • *Narrative* • *Expository*	
Content/Themes/Ideas	
Strategies for Making Meaning	
Levels of Comprehension • *Literal* • *Inferential* • *Applied*	
Prior Knowledge • *Linguistic* • *Cultural* • *Experiential*	
Literary Features/Devices • *Perspective/Point of view* • *Dialog* • *Chronology*	
Language Features/Devices • *Vocabulary* • *Idioms, figurative language* • *Structures and patterns* • *Complexity*	
Language Cohesion • *Reference* • *Substitution* • *Ellipses* • *Conjunctions* • *Lexical cohesion*	
Engagement/Opportunities to • *Talk* • *Reflect*	
Book/Print Features • *Length/Organization* • *Font* • *Layout* • *Visuals*	
Additional Supports/Challenges	

—Adapted from Messiano, 2002, and Fountas and Pinnell, 2002.

SELECTING TEXT FOR ENGLISH LEARNERS

Select texts with:

♦ Repetitive language that encourages students to join in.

♦ A repetitive event that builds to a culminating event. Once students understand the structure of the repetitive event, they transfer this understanding to each repetition.

♦ Universal themes that are age-appropriate and relevant.

♦ Clear print and well-designed pages.

♦ Authentic and natural language models.

♦ Content and language that may be challenging but are accessible through specialized teacher supports and scaffolds.

♦ Content and language that extend students' understanding of reading and the world.

♦ Content that is interesting and fun to read.

Additional Features of "Considerate" Nonfiction Texts

Select nonfiction texts with:

♦ Clear and consistent text organization.

♦ Clear text markings and signaling devices. The text is structured to clearly present devices such as titles, headings, captions, topic sentences, and text cohesion.

♦ Appropriate content density. New topics are well spaced and contain sufficient elaboration to make them understandable.

♦ Supportive instructional and reference devices such as a table of contents, glossary, index, graphic overviews, diagrams, and summaries.

♦ Visuals that are clear and logical and enhance understanding of the text.

—Adapted from Pauline Gibbons, *Scaffolding Language, Scaffolding Learning,*
Heinemann, 2002. Used with permission.

The Language Experience Approach (LEA)

The language experience approach is a technique that naturally extends oral language development into reading and writing, using and validating the student's own authentic language. Comprehension and self-esteem are assured because the student's own language serves as the foundation on which literacy is built.[32] This approach has several noted advantages for English learners in particular:[33]

- "Core" reading material is familiar, relevant, and nonthreatening since it originated from the students.
- Student's language has value and serves to further literacy development.
- Value of life experiences, interests, ideas, and culture is demonstrated both intrinsically and as a source of learning in the classroom.
- Integration of listening, speaking, reading, and writing is demonstrated.
- A shared "background" is assured by the shared experience. It does not assume a single cultural or linguistic background.
- LEA can be modified for students at all stages of language proficiency.
- Conventional use of language (including mechanics) is modeled.

Step by Step: The Language Experience Approach

1. *Share and discuss an experience.* The experience could be a science experiment, field trip, or literature selection. Allow plenty of time for discussion. This step is crucial in developing key vocabulary and concepts.

2. *Lead the group in dictating a story.* Encourage students to describe the experience. Individuals can contribute words, phrases, and/or sentences. Record the story on chart paper (or on an overhead or the chalkboard). Encourage all students to contribute. The stories can be recorded as running narratives *(We went to the library. We walked by many houses.)* or as a series of quotes *(Lia said, "I found books about the United States." Tommy said, "I found books about South America.")*

3. *Read the story and consider revisions.* Read and discuss the story. Ask students if they want to make changes, additions, or deletions. Model and involve students in thinking through these decisions. Make changes as suggested. (Sentences on chart paper can be cut apart and physically reordered.)

4. *Read and reread the story.* Lead students in a choral reading of the story. Continue with echo reading, encouraging individuals or partners to read portions of the story.

5. *Extend the experience.* Use the story to extend literacy and explore aspects of print with activities such as the following:
   - Students illustrate the story and attach illustrations to the chart.
   - Students create a big-book version of the story.
   - Make a copy the story for each student. Students illustrate, read, and take home their own copy.
   - Students adapt a story into a play or reader's theater.
   - Students add dialog to a story.

> **TIP** Note on errors: As a general rule, you should record students' words exactly as they are spoken. However, when a speech "error" occurs, ask the student, as if clarifying meaning, "Is this what I should write?" as you model the standard form. For example:
>
> *Student:* We goed to the store.
> *Teacher:* Yes, we went to the store. Shall I write, "We went to the store"?
>
> The concern here is to avoid confusing students in the group who have already acquired the irregular grammatical structure of *went*. The teacher, the language authority, should be viewed as one who consistently models the standard to which students are aiming.

TIP LEA is a good way for you to develop phonemic awareness, phonics, and other conventions of print.

- Explore aspects of print. For example:
  —Students find and/or identify matching words.
  —Students identify letters, words, sentences, capitalization, and punctuation.
  —Copy the story on sentence strips. Students match the strips to story sentences and/or order the sentences in story sequence, using the chart story as a visual reference.
  —Make word cards. Students match the card to the word in the story and/or order the word cards to create sentences from the story.
  —Students add words to their own personal word banks, dictionaries, or writing notebooks.

Phonemic Awareness/Phonics

Effective teachers interweave these activities within their instruction and, above all, ensure that phonics teaching is not done apart from connected, informative, engaging text.

—Anne Sweet, *State of the Art* [34]

TIP Refer to the "Modeled Writing" section on page 76. This is an excellent tool for developing phonemic awareness. For example, in writing "The Daily News":

Teacher: Today is Monday. I will write this sentence. What sounds do you hear in *Today*? (Teacher assists students in listening for the sounds within words, then records the matching letters/words.)

TIP The following strategies are particularly helpful for developing phonemic/phonics awareness:

- Language experience (see page 65)
- Guided reading (see page 56)
- Modeled/Shared writing (see page 76)
- Interactive writing (see page 77)
- Developmental writing (see page 80)
- Re-creations and innovations (see page 84)

Phonemic awareness involves a student's ability to discern the sounds in a word and then distinguish between words based on the sounds. Phonics skill, identifying and applying the sound/symbol of written language, emerges from a foundation of phonemic awareness. Phonics and phonemic awareness can be difficult for English learners who are also learning that the sounds that carry meaning in their home language may or may not carry meaning in English. Effective beginning reading instruction for English learners *must* contain a balance of strategies and activities designed to develop English phonemic awareness and phonics within meaningful contexts.

Phonics is an important part of a balanced literacy program. It is the graphophonic cueing system that allows students to verify their reading and decode known but previously unread words. Rather than using isolated drills or worksheets that carry little meaning (particularly for English learners who may not know the names of the ten pictures on the page that are supposed to represent *m*), *phonics strategies are developed and explicitly taught through contextualized reading and writing activities.* Contextualized activities are often embedded in instructional strategies and approaches, and they can take many forms:

- Writing poetry
- Innovations/re-creations
- Identifying matching letters and words from a group story or daily news
- Identifying sound or spelling patterns
- Singing and writing lyrics to songs

As Bobbi Fisher writes, " . . . If we as teachers want children to apply their letter and sound knowledge, we must demonstrate how to do this strategically as we read." [35]

As with many activities for English language learners, it is appropriate that phonics instruction be made explicit. The context and students' background knowledge must set the stage for focused instruction. Beginning phonics instruction may be developed in the following ways.

Developing Phonemic Awareness

Phonemic awareness begins early. Students benefit from listening to stories and poems, engaging in activities such as finger-plays, songs, clapping out words, and repeating rhymes that direct their attention to the sounds of language.[36] Phonemic awareness continues to develop as students learn the alphabet and develop understanding and skills in phonics.

Although most students master phonemic awareness in the primary grades, it is not uncommon for English learners to arrive at our schools in the upper grades with limited or incomplete understandings of English sounds. For these students, explicit instruction in phonemic awareness that is a small part of a more intensive literacy program is of great value. In its publication *Strategic Teaching and Learning: Standards-Based Instruction to Promote Content Literacy in Grades Four Through Twelve,* the California Department of Education recommends that for older learners, phonemic awareness training should occupy no more than 10 minutes at the beginning of a lesson.[37] A sequence of activities shifting from attention to phonemes to letter/sound relationships is suggested:

1. *Phoneme production/replication:* Students distinguish and produce the sounds of English with particular attention to similar sounds such as /b/ and /p/.

2. *Phoneme isolation:* Students identify specific sounds at the beginning, middle, and end of a word.

3. *Phoneme segmentation and counting:* Students identify each of the sounds (phonemes) they hear in a spoken word, such as /c/, /a/, /t/. Students count the speech sounds in words and then clap out and identify the number of syllables in their names and other words.

4. *Phoneme blending:* Students blend a set of sounds together to form a word.

5. *Rhyming words:* Students identify and produce rhyming words.

6. *Phoneme deletion:* Students say words, leaving off the initial or final sounds, and blend. For example, *band* becomes *and* or *ripe* becomes *stripe.*

7. *Phoneme substitution:* Students change the beginning, ending, and then medial sound to form a new word. For example, *cat* becomes *bat* or *can* becomes *cat.*

Learning the Alphabet

This early, important step can be easily accomplished through rhyme, song, or chants. In addition, abundant and varied activities in which students identify, match, and form letters, as well as alphabet games (e.g., Bingo, computer games, card games) all contribute to learning the alphabet.

Developing Sound and Symbol Awareness

Students who have had many opportunities to hear and play with the alphabet and the sounds of English are better prepared to develop sound/symbol awareness. This process, however, is more complex than it seems. English does not contain a simple one-to-one correspondence between each letter and each sound. English contains many more meaningful sounds (phonemes—about 40) than most languages. In addition, many of these sounds can be represented by many symbols. For example, the *f* sound can be represented by the letters *f, ff,* or *ph.*[38]

TIP Use language students have already acquired as tools for developing phonemic awareness. Fully develop the meaning of songs, chants, and so on prior to identifying or matching specific sounds within the words.

TIP The key idea is to help students hear the sounds of English so that they can quickly and easily take words apart, put sounds together to form words, and manipulate and reconfigure sounds to make new words.

TIP Use the "Alphabet Song" or the "Alphabet Cheer" for older students. Make alphabet cards for students to hold as they sing. Use alphabet stamps and magnetic letters.

TIP Use a variety of alphabet books to immerse students in the sounds of English. Distribute the books, having students look up specific letters (for example, "Find the page that includes the first letter of your name"). Discuss and compare the entries for the letter in the various books.

Have students make their own class alphabet for the wall or for a book. Cut out very large letters. Assign a student group to each letter and have each group make illustrations and/or cut from magazines pictures beginning with the sound and paste them to the letter cut-out. Arrange and display the letters, or assemble them in a book.

Overreliance on the strategy of sounding out words tends to slow down the reading process and hinders fluency. English learners in particular are also apt to lose the meaning of the text.

A blank word-form chart appears in the Resource Pages. Refer to page 131.

For English learners still learning to make meaning out of the whole sounds of English, it is very important that instruction be embedded in meaningful activities. Activities focusing on encoding (writing) and decoding (sounding it out) are valuable when a variety of other clues can be drawn from the context as needed.

Using the Home Language

Although students can and do learn to read in a second language, research confirms the value of providing initial literacy instruction in the language students understand best, their home language. The strategies and skills developed will transfer to reading in English.[39]

Word Study

Understanding phonics and phonemic awareness is a key element of word study—the study of words and how they work. Through word study, students learn how words work, in essence, how they are taken apart and put together. They learn to see the chunks or patterns that constitute words in English and apply this learning to "solve" new words in reading and writing. Students apply their learning at the letter (phoneme) level, chunk level (sound patterns), and word level (known words). To solve a word, efficient readers tend to use these strategies in the order presented:

- *Know* the word: The word is known by sight. This is the most efficient strategy and requires students to be familiar and fluent with words.
- *Chunk* the word: Students should use this strategy to tackle an unfamiliar, long, or multisyllabic word. They look for patterns or chunks that are known and apply them to the new word (for example, *ent, as, ing, ise, ight, pre, ment, tion, sion*).
- *Sound out* the word: Students sound out each letter of the word and blend the sounds together to say the word. This is the least efficient strategy, and it should be reserved for solving only very short words.

Attending to the relationship between specific types of words or word categories supports more proficient English learners in vocabulary development and in refining aspects of grammar.

Word Forms

An often confusing or overlooked aspect of English is the ways in which words change meaning—and often change form—in specific grammatical contexts. For example, the word *hope* can be used in a sentence as both a noun and a verb. In addition, there are groups of related words that are similar but vary depending on the grammatical function they serve in a sentence. For example, the words *expectation, expectant, expect,* and *expectantly*, although closely related in terms of the core concept, are each used in grammatically distinct contexts.

Understanding the relationship between word forms adds to the linguistic repertoire students need to expand vocabulary and manipulate the grammar and structure of language. Charting these relationships provides a visual in which patterns and relationships are made evident. The chart

WORD FORMS			
Noun	**Adjective**	**Verb**	**Adverb**
confidence	confident		confidently
	soft	soften	softly
purpose	purposeful		purposefully
happiness	happy		happily
caution	cautious		cautiously
hope	hopeful	hope	hopefully
appreciation	appreciative	appreciate	
expectation	expectant	expect	expectantly
enthusiasm	enthusiastic	enthuse	enthusiastically
mess	messy	mess	messily

TIP As students add to the chart, help them analyze the patterns and relationships that emerge (for example, many adverbs end in *ly* and tend to relate to the structure of adjectives; words ending in *tion* are usually nouns). Discuss how this can help them solve and construct new words in English.

above or the blank word-form chart on page 131 can be posted on the wall and added to as word-form "families" are identified in a text. This chart serves as a resource for students to expand—as well as see the connectedness of—language and vocabulary. Students can devise their own personal word-form chart on a sheet of paper.[40]

Signal Words

English contains a variety of linguistic markers—key words or phrases—that signal meaning. Signal words establish a context for meaning and frequently provide readers with clues as to what they can anticipate in a text. For example:

- *She wanted to go, <u>but</u> she couldn't.*
  The word *but* signals a change. The reader anticipates a new direction in the text.

- *She wanted to go, <u>so</u> she called to accept the invitation.*
  The word *so* signals continuance. The reader anticipates that the text will continue its current direction.

- *He eats only certain vegetables, <u>such as</u> carrots, peas, and corn.*
  The phrase *such as* signals example. The reader anticipates that the text will provide examples.

Many of these signal words and phrases are conjunctions. Readers must properly interpret signal words to read with fluency and comprehension. Writers must possess a command of these important words to bring fluency, order, and cohesion to their writing.

As students increase in reading and language fluency, word study gradually shifts to the sentence, paragraph, and whole text. Students learn how words are combined and manipulated to form grammatical English sentences and narratives. Students better understand the English texts they read and develop skills that enable them to construct coherent and cohesive sentences, paragraphs, and whole texts.

In word-form charts, do not feel obligated to include words that, although correct, are obscure or potentially confusing (for example, *appreciatively*).

Note how the following sentence, while grammatically correct, does not make sense:

She wanted to go, but she called to accept the invitation.

In this example, the "signals" were crossed!

See page 70 for a chart of signal words and phrases that can be posted in the classroom for easy reference.

SIGNAL WORDS AND PHRASES

Words that signal sequence and temporal order

first, last	next	before	later
second, etc.	until	after	finally
preceding	ultimate	since	then

Words that signal lists or addition of ideas

also	in addition	moreover	besides
another	and	further	furthermore

Words that signal definition

refers to	means	that is (i.e.)	is the same as
consists of	synonymous with	stands for	in other words

Words that signal example

for instance	such as	like	for example (e.g.)
including	to illustrate	case	case in point

Words that signal analysis

consider	investigate	this means	analyze
suggests	examine	scrutinize	explore

Words that signal comparison

also	in the same way	just like	likewise
corresponds	similarly	just as	equally

Words that signal contrast

in contrast	on the other hand	however	whereas
and yet	as opposed to	different	varies or differs

Words that signal a cause-effect relationship

because	therefore	if (then)	hence
as a result	consequently	due to	thus
then, so	leads to	accordingly	since

Words that signal a change in direction

but	although	even though	though
even if	while	however	nevertheless

Words that signal conclusion

in conclusion	close	wind up	wrap up
conclude	end	finish	summarize

—Adapted from Kinsella, 2001b, and Harvey and Goudvis, 2000.

Cohesion and Cohesive Devices

Language, both spoken and written, maintains its natural flow because it is held together by cohesive ties. Cohesion differentiates a string of unrelated sentences from a group of sentences that flow together in a coherent whole.

Proficient readers are able to carry meaning over chunks of text. Less proficient readers tend not to do this but rather to focus on the meaning of smaller units of text such as single words or short phrases. The result is a breakdown of meaning as students continue through the text. The ability to carry meaning all the way through a text depends on being able to process cohesive devices between and within sentences.

While native speakers of English may have an intuitive understanding of how cohesion operates, English learners may not have fully developed this understanding. Explicitly pointing out and teaching students how to use these links will help students sustain meaning and better understand how English works in all its domains: listening, speaking, reading, and writing.

Cohesion involves five areas, each of which present unique challenges to English learners.[41]

1. *Reference:* Reference involves devices in a text that refer to something else in the text. Referents signal the need to look somewhere else in the text, usually pointing back to something or someone previously mentioned. They include pronouns such as *he, she, them, it,* and *those.*

   The weather was perfect. Susan hoped it would remain this way. <u>Her</u> friend was visiting from out of town and <u>she</u> wanted <u>her</u> to enjoy <u>it</u>.

   In this example, the reader must recognize the relationship between the references (*it, this, her, she*) and the referents (*weather, perfect, Susan, friend*). It is not uncommon for a short section of text to contain several references or for a given character to be referred to in several different ways over the course of the narrative (e.g., *Daniel: he, his, the brother, concerned friend, new, the student*).

2. *Substitution:* Substitution is a device in a text that allows the writer to avoid the need to repeat a word or element. Another word or phrase is substituted.

   Sara got a new video game for her birthday. <u>I did too</u>.

   Other possible substitutions for this example include the following: <u>*This*</u> *was her third. Her <u>other one</u> was broken.*

3. *Ellipses:* Ellipses can usually be thought of as omissions. The use of this device allows the writer and requires the reader to assume certain information that is not explicit in the text.

   Some people live in houses and some don't (<u>live in houses</u>).
   He changed his clothes, (<u>he</u>) brushed his teeth, and (<u>he</u>) went to bed.

   In each example, the underlined word(s) are omitted from the text and must be supplied by the reader.

Creating a coherent paragraph is similar to having a conversation with the reader, but the writing must be much clearer and more explicit as it must carry context and meaning without the benefit of immediate feedback from the reader.

It is not necessary or even advisable to require students to name each device. Rather, help them develop the awareness and ability to understand text cohesion as well as incorporate the devices in their own writing.

Can you identify the cohesive device used in this paragraph about reference?

English learners may not see the connection between the referent and what it is referring to or be able to follow this thread through a longer text.

Students may begin a written piece with a pronoun that has no referent and is therefore incomprehensible to a reader (*You wrote, "She came over . . . ." Who does "She" refer to?*). In this case, the student must learn that the reader needs a context or more specifically that a pronoun must refer to a preceding noun.

English learners may not understand that the substitution *I did too* actually means *I also (too) got a new video game for my birthday.*

English learners may not recognize any omissions and will therefore be unable to supply the missing word, making comprehension difficult. They may also be unable to apply this device to their writing, resulting in writing that sounds redundant or wordy.

English learners will benefit from recognizing conjunctions and understanding how they trigger meaning.

> **TIP** Watch for students' use and understanding of conjunctions. The student who reads *The light was red, so the car kept going* without stopping to check meaning has missed the point as meaning hinges on understanding the word *so*.

See page 70 for categories of conjunctions that can support students' comprehension of text and their efforts in writing.

English learners may need support to draw on their prior knowledge in order to recognize lexical connections in text and also to elicit a variety of related vocabulary that can be incorporated in their own writing.

"Because cohesion is not a very visible language system and is one which is intuitively understood by native speakers, it is easy to overlook the difficulties it may cause for second language learners." (Pauline Gibbons[43])

4. *Conjunctions:* Conjunctions are devices that significantly influence meaning in text. They typically are key words that link and organize ideas and also help the reader anticipate and interpret what comes next in text. Pauline Gibbons provides the following examples of conjunctions that help readers predict how the sentences are likely to end:

Although the light was red, the car (kept going).
The light was red, but the car (kept going).
Because the light was red, the car (stopped).
The light was red, so the car (stopped).[42]

In these examples, the basic content and key vocabulary remained the same. What changed, and significantly impacted meaning, were the conjunctions. Conjunctions include devices that are additive (*and, further, also*), expository (*that is, in other words*), comparative (*like, similarly, as*), or contrastive (*however, because*) and devices that mark time (*first, next, later*).

5. *Lexical cohesion:* Lexical cohesion is a device used to link vocabulary and often utilizes synonyms to enhance literary style and flow.

The sky slowly darkened with the setting sun. He stopped what he was doing to watch the sunset. These twilight moments were often his favorite as he watched the sun slowly drop into the blue Pacific.

In this example the underlined words are related to sunset. The related words hold the text together and make it more stylistically pleasing than repeating the same word over and over.

Instruction on cohesion should be explicit but should always be provided in the context of authentic reading and writing experiences. Instructional approaches—including shared reading, guided reading, reading and writing conference, shared and modeled writing, and guided language study—provide many opportunities to meaningfully develop aspects of cohesion.

Understanding how cohesion works in an English text will enable teachers to do the following:

- Identify possible reasons why students do not understand the text.
- Recognize potential challenges in the text—even text that initially may appear simple.
- Identify reasons why students' writing does not sound fluent, even if it is grammatically correct with no obvious errors.
- Determine appropriate reading and writing strategies for students.

Understanding how cohesion works in an English text will enable *students* to do the following:

- Navigate the text with understanding, carrying meaning through the whole text.
- Refer to what has been read and anticipate what is to come.
- Recognize the organization and structure of the text.
- Build a stronger conceptual framework for the text by seeing connections and relationships.
- Read and write with greater fluency.

The development of deeper understanding of how cohesion in English works in speech and text will greatly enhance students' ability to function at high levels of English proficiency.

Guided Language Study

Guided language study (also referred to as focused ELD) is designed to promote enhanced and purposeful language instruction. Students are grouped with others at a similar language proficiency level with similar instructional needs. Guided language study is connected to daily classroom instruction. It both supports and builds on key concepts and content being taught through literacy instruction or through other subjects.

Through interactions and careful observation of students, teachers interpret what they are seeing in order to identify specific language needs that can be supported or directly taught. Teachers ask themselves these questions:

- *Do I know and understand what I am observing?*
- *Is the issue related to any of these aspects:*

    Vocabulary
    Language structures, patterns, or cohesive devices
    Background knowledge
    Conceptual/cognitive demand of the content itself
    The reading process

Teachers identify not only the need but also its underlying cause. It cannot be assumed that reading challenges for English learners are related only to vocabulary and language structures. Effective instruction must reflect the actual need (cause)—not simply the deficiency (symptom). In guided language study, teaching and learning are based on authentic language at a student's point of need—the real language issues needed to move students to higher levels of proficiency.

Directed Reading-Thinking

Directed reading-thinking activities are used to guide and coach students to draw meaning from print as they read segments of the text and respond to predicting and verifying questions. This process replicates, as closely as possible, the way the mind processes text.[44] The goal of directed reading-thinking is to make explicit the connection between print and meaning and to help students develop meaning-making strategies. *Directed reading-thinking is an important tool for selected pieces of literature, but it should be used sparingly.* It complements strategies in which students routinely read and hear whole works straight through. The process can be used by either reading to students or having them read independently or with partners.

Step by Step: Directed Reading-Thinking Activities

1. *Prepare the text.* Preread the text and identify the segments that contain the major events of the story. Try to divide the story into segments that will promote deeper thinking.

Teachers may preview text students will encounter in a subsequent read aloud or shared experience, focus on specific grammatical points, or review and extend prior learning.

Guided language study enables teachers to tailor instruction to meet the specific needs of their students.

Guided language study is also informed by and incorporates student writing.

TIP Do not use this strategy with every piece of reading. It is also important that students hear stories straight through, as a whole. Select reading pieces that can be presented in short segments and lend themselves to predictions.

2. *Prepare the students.* Prepare students for reading the text by developing background concepts and language. Show the book cover and/or read the title. Encourage students to describe the cover and predict what the story will be about. Ask predicting questions:

   - *What do you think this story will be about?*
   - *What characters do you think will be in the story? Why do you think so? Be specific. Record predictions for later reference.*

3. *Read a segment of the text.* Read the first story segment. Have students compare their predictions to the actual reading passage to either verify their predictions or identify the parts of their predictions that were inaccurate or are still unknown. For example:

   - *Were we right about the story/characters?*
   - *Do we know yet?*

4. *Repeat and continue the process.* Ask more predicting questions based on the reading. Record the predictions. Read the next segment. Ask verifying questions.

5. *Review and reread the whole story.* After completing the story, discuss the predictions, reactions, and impressions. Read or have students reread the story as a whole.

Directed Viewing-Thinking

The directed reading-thinking procedure can be adapted for use with videos. The purpose is the same, drawing meaning from and interacting with a story. Follow the steps listed previously, pausing the video to verify and predict.

Observable Reading Characteristics

Students who are beginning readers progress through reading in roughly predictable ways. Some of these early reading characteristics are included on page 75, Observable Reading Characteristics. Observing student reading behaviors provides important insights into what students are now able to do, and what they are learning to do, as readers. This information can be used by teachers to inform the next instructional steps for students.

TIP Identify videos that would lend themselves to directed viewing-thinking.

OBSERVABLE READING CHARACTERISTICS

General Reading Behaviors

- Chooses an appropriate book: familiar or unfamiliar.
- Exhibits readinglike behavior with no sequential text attention and uses own language. (Uses picture cues and experiential knowledge.)
- Exhibits readinglike behavior approximating the language of the text. (Print is constant.)
- Exhibits readinglike behavior, approximating the language of the text and using directional print conventions. (Print carries the message.)
- Tracks print 1:1 with finger or eyes.
- Understands the concept of a letter.
- Understands the concept of a word.
- Locates specific words in text by rereading and confirming with phonological and visual cues.
- Knows some words by sight.
- Uses the cueing systems:
    Semantic cues
    Syntactic cues
    Phonological cues
    Visual cues
- Integrates the cueing systems to gain meaning from text.
- Prepares to read orally by reading silently.

Reading Strategies

- Expects the text to make sense and sound right.
- Reads for meaning—not to identify words.
- Processes chunks of language.
- Makes predictions about text.
- Self-corrects when predictions are unsatisfactory. (Cross-checks cueing systems.)
- Employs self-correcting strategies when in difficulty:
    Rereads sentence from the beginning.
    Reads on to end of sentence.
    Uses beginning letters or cues.
    Uses picture cues, then guesses.
    Uses phonetic or structural analysis.

Comprehension

- Retells story or passage in own words.
- Talks about the characters.
- Recalls the main idea.
- Recalls the supporting details.
- Understands story sequence.
- Understands story structure.
- Makes inferences about the story and supports them with prior knowledge or evidence from the text.

Reading Conference

- *Choosing a book:* "Find a book to read to me that is just right for you, not too hard and not too easy."
- *Beginning of conference:* "While you are reading, I will be listening and writing down all that you show me you know about reading."
- *Comprehension:* "Now tell me all that you remember about the story from beginning to end."

Books I've Read

Name: _____

Title	Date	:)	:|	:(

Reprinted from "Practical Authentic Assessment" by D. Fisette, 1993, p. 4, by permission of *The California Reader.*

Modeled Writing

Modeled writing allows students to see the teacher as a proficient writer and a reader. Teachers demonstrate and model the writing process, including adding, revising, asking questions, and clarifying purposes for writing. Teachers may also employ a "think-aloud" strategy as they write, describing the thinking and decision making adult writers go through to compose a text.[45] This technique can be adapted to any age level and and can be used to focus on any writing strategy that can be demonstrated or modeled through actual writing. The teacher models the process on chart paper or the overhead projector. For example:

- *I am going to write a letter to my friend Marcy, so I use the common greeting, "Dear Marcy."* (Teacher writes "Dear Marcy" on the overhead.)

- *I haven't written to her for a while, so I'd better apologize for not writing. I have to leave a space and then write.* (Teacher leaves a space and begins thinking "out loud" by saying what is being written: *I am sorry I haven't written to you for so long. I have been really busy.)*

The teacher continues thinking aloud and then writing. This explicit demonstration of writing, along with the thought processes used by the proficient writer, supports students as they begin writing or are learning new aspects of more sophisticated writing.

Shared Writing

Shared writing is similar to modeled writing, with students taking a more active role. This technique provides an opportunity for all students to develop their understanding of written language and successfully participate in the writing process. Teachers invite student participation and active engagement as they demonstrate and model new writing skills, strategies, and language patterns. Students and teachers share the task of creating a readable text that can be used again.

A sample shared writing experience might include the following:

1. The teacher demonstrates by modeling a short piece, perhaps a simple story of a personal event.
2. The teacher elicits "help" from students to model and reinforce specific aspects of the writing such as language structures, word chunks and spellings, or descriptive language.
3. The teacher reads the piece, asking for ideas to improve the writing—making it clearer or more interesting.
4. Students and teacher read the piece together.

The shared experience can be extended by having students practice writing on their own. The sample shared writing experience might continue as follows:

5. Students are asked to think about the story or sentences they want to write, and get the actual words "in their heads." Students are encouraged to talk about the story with a partner.

6. Students share the story with their partners and the teacher and then begin the writing.

7. Students later share their writing with the group.

Interactive Writing

Interactive writing is a teaching method in which children and teacher negotiate what they are going to write and then share the pen to construct the message.

—Stanley Swartz, Adria Klein, and Rebecca Shook,
Interactive Writing and Interactive Editing[46]

Interactive writing is a process that reveals how written language works. It involves the explicit demonstration of writing and writing strategies as students and teachers co-construct text. This approach is particularly beneficial for early writers and English learners who are new to English because interactive writing is based on oral language. Students are immersed in meaningful talk as they negotiate meaning and what they will write. Students are further supported by the teacher as they individually "share the pen" by contributing letters, words, or phrases to the written piece.[47]

> Interactive writing provides abundant opportunities for direct and explicit instruction in phonemic awareness and phonics instruction within a meaningful context.
>
> Oral language development is a key feature of interactive writing and serves as a rich source for the written piece.

Writing Through Talk and Illustration

Writing through talk and illustration capitalizes on talk and conversation to bring detail, fluency, and depth to students' early writing. The writing task can be approached in two ways:

1. Students select a previous piece that they can rewrite or enhance.

2. Students create a new piece.

Students are led through the basic steps:

1. *Talk the picture:* Teachers give each student one to three sheets of paper. Students talk with each other and the teacher, discussing what they can draw on each of the pages to tell their story. Teachers coach and support students in providing rich descriptions, and they ask questions that will lead to detailed illustrations and a coherent story line. *What does the girl wear to the party? What color is her dress? What color are her new shoes? Does she bring a present?*

2. *The picture:* Students illustrate the story they have described. Students are reminded to include the key elements, meaningful details, and any colors that they described. The richer the details, the richer the conversation and the writing will be.

> This is a particularly effective technique for English learners because students are immersed in meaningful talk at each step. Teachers support and extend students' language.

3. *Talk the writing:* Students discuss, describe, and "read" the picture story. Teachers coach students in how to use "story language" to read the picture. Teachers model and support students in formulating sentences for each "scene" that will make up the story, reminding students to include the rich language and detail they discussed and illustrated. Students practice saying the story aloud.

4. *The writing:* Students then write the picture story. Students are again reminded to utilize the rich and descriptive language they practiced.

5. *The share:* Students read their stories to the group. Students ask questions and compare the completed story to the previous discussion.

Variation: Students illustrate a book jacket or favorite scene from a story, adding the necessary details to capture the key story elements and theme.

Independent Writing

Independent writing provides an opportunity for students to write. It is included within writing workshop and may also occur at other times. Independent writing provides opportunities for students to practice the writing strategies and skills they have learned. Students are encouraged to write for authentic purposes and use a variety of styles. Teachers confer with students to monitor progress and to provide targeted support. Students are encouraged to publish selected pieces.

Process Writing

Process writing is an approach that encourages English learners to engage in writing even as they are developing the companion literacy skills of reading and speaking.[48] This flexible framework is useful for students at all developmental stages. The five steps, summarized in the following section, can be adapted to meet the needs of individual students and different writing situations. In real life and in the classroom, many types of writing are complete after the first draft. Only selected pieces are fully developed through all five stages.

Step by Step: Process Writing

1. *Prewriting.* Prewriting experiences help students tap into background knowledge and experience and develop the need and desire to write. Prewriting activities involve students in collecting a resource pool of possible writing ideas, vocabulary, and language structures. These experiences can include a shared field trip, cooking, discussions, brainstorming, creating a graphic organizer, and responding to literature.

2. *Drafting.* Students can jot down their thoughts using scribbles, drawings, letters, or more conventional writing. The purpose here is to get ideas and thoughts down on paper. Spelling, mechanics, and structure take a backseat to fluency of ideas. Students approximate standard language usage.

3. *Sharing and responding to writing.* Students share their writing with a partner, group, or teacher. They can do so informally, collaboratively, or as part of a writer's conference. Students respond to writing in supportive and helpful ways by modeling positive responses and thoughtful questions. A writer's conference may include focused attention on specific skills or strategies.

4. *Revising writing.* Students incorporate feedback from responses and make corrections, additions, or deletions to their writing. This stage concerns itself with both content—the flow and communication of thought—and mechanics.

5. *Publishing.* Publishing is the culmination of a significant work. There are numerous ways in which students can publish their work: posters, charts, letters or e-mail messages, brochures, and books of all sorts—big books, little books, accordion books, puppet or shape books, pop-up books, or bound books.

These processes can be incorporated and supported in the writing workshop.

TIP Prewriting is a crucial step for English learners. You may spend a great deal of extra time developing the language and planning the writing.

TIP Determine the purpose of students' writing. Use the purpose to determine the degree to which the piece will be taken through the writing process. Do not expect or require all pieces of writing to be letter perfect. English learners in particular need opportunities to develop fluency in writing, just as they do in speech.

Writing Workshop

What I know about writing has to do with where you put your heart.

—Nasdijj[49]

We should never forget that the central kernel of our work is not writing but real kids—their voices, passions, imagination, their original slant on the world.

—Ralph Fletcher and Joann Portalupi (eds.), *Writing Workshop*[50]

The writing workshop model is similar to the reading workshop in that it organizes instruction and supports students in their learning. Students are engaged in daily writing and interactions with others because the writing workshop replicates the processes real writers use. Teachers begin with brief direct instruction on a specific writing strategy or skill (a mini-lesson). Students then write. Teachers check in with students, monitoring and providing guidance and feedback (writing conferences). Finally, students have a chance to debrief with the whole group and share their work (share).[51]

Through the writing workshop, students come to see themselves as writers.

Step by Step: Writing Workshop

1. *Mini-lesson:* Mini-lessons are short, focused, and direct, providing an opportunity to introduce a specific idea, strategy, or skill that seems relevant to the group of students at a particular time. Students may practice the strategy or skill during the mini-lesson. For instance, the teacher might say: *Select a page in your writer's notebook that has a strong sense of place.* However, students are not limited to focusing on only this strategy during writing time.

2. *Writing with conferring:* This is the heart of the writing workshop. Students engage in authentic writing projects. They plan, draft, reflect, reread/proofread, and discuss. The teacher confers with students as they write, providing guidance, direction, and teaching points.

3. *Share:* This is a special time for students to share their writing. Teachers often designate an "author's chair" for this purpose. Teachers coach and guide students to question and respond to the writing. Students can share writing at all stages of the process. It is this shared experience that helps students to understand the layers and processes involved in writing.

The share experience may be conducted with the whole class or a small response group. Older students may benefit from regular response partners who can listen and provide feedback as a piece evolves over time. Students in response groups will also need coaching and teacher support.

Fletcher and Portalupi identify typical mini-lesson categories:

- *Procedural*—the operational and logistical aspects of the workshop, including materials and conference locations.
- *Writer's process*—topic selection, exploration, and organization; text organization and structure.
- *Qualities of good writing*—literary techniques, development of place, audience, point of view, strong language, leads, endings, and so on.
- *Editing skills*—developing understanding of print conventions, spelling, and grammatical structures.[52]

TIP Encourage students to analyze and respond to writing by asking questions:

- *What did the writer do well?*
- *What questions do you have? What did you learn?*

Writer's Notebook: Collecting Ideas for Writing

Writers are like other people, except for at least one important difference. Other people have daily thoughts and feelings, notice this sky or that smell, but they don't do much about it. All those thoughts, feelings, sensations, and opinions pass through them like the air they breathe. Not writers. Writers react.

—Ralph Fletcher, *A Writer's Notebook*[53]

Writers get ideas everywhere—usually away from their desks: in the car, standing in line at the bank or grocery store, watching a baseball game. A writer's reaction to ideas is to write them down.

A writer's notebook is a tool used by writers to record their ideas and collect their bits of writing. As students go about living their lives, they are on the lookout for new ideas:

- A close observation of something (that notes an object's color, texture, smell, and so on)
- Any interesting observation
- Part of an overheard conversation
- Dialog, phrases, or quotes from TV, books, music
- Things to wonder about
- Everyday, ordinary events
- Family stories
- Something remembered from the past

Thoughts or fragments of thoughts and ideas are written in the writer's notebook. In addition, more purposeful entries might be included. If students are studying a certain genre or particular type of writing, they are asked to include entries that could provide material for that genre.

The writer's notebook is a personal writing sourcebook for students. Over time, students enter ideas and bits of writing often referred to as *seed ideas* that can later be used as a source of inspiration for *writing projects*. Students select a seed idea they wish to pursue through drafting, revising, and so on, until the idea is a finished piece of writing.[54]

Writing is about decision: deciding on wording, style, plot, structure. The writer's notebook is also about choice. Seed ideas can quickly fill a notebook, but students will need to make decisions about what they wish to pursue as a writing project. As students pay attention to seed ideas and make decisions about what to pursue as a writing project, they are encouraged to think and act like writers.

Journals and Learning Logs

Journals and learning logs are places where students record what they are pondering and learning in and out of school. In them, students may make sketches, drawings, and notes; record observations and reflections; and interact through print with the teacher or peers. Journals and learning logs allow students to clarify and record ideas for later use. Although similar to a writer's notebook, journals and learning logs tend to be more focused and topical, such as a math or science learning log in which students record findings and learning around the subject or a journal in which students record daily experiences.

Interactive journals allow a running dialog with the teacher or peer. Comments written by the teacher in an interactive journal should be authentic, specific, and brief.

Emergent/Developmental Writing

Students learn to write by writing. They progress through the stages of writing just as they progress though the stages of speech and reading. Teachers must create a classroom environment that encourages emerging writers to experiment and grow. Instructional practices that promote this environment include the following:

Developing a writer's notebook is very freeing to English learners. They too collect seed ideas and record them in their notebooks in ways that make sense to them. This provides practice and fluency in writing without the constraints of conventions and structures. When a particular seed idea is selected to pursue as a writing project, students then attend to language and writing conventions.

A writer's notebook for very young students may simply consist of a folder in which writing and ideas are collected. Older students may use a binder, notebook, folder, or any system that makes sense to them. It is important, however, that the ideas be contained in such a way that they are not easily lost.

"Literacy allows us to find the life of the intellect within the details of ordinary life." (Lucy McCormick Calkins [55])

TIP Encourage all students to write in their journals on a daily basis.

TIP Have very beginning students bring in environmental print that they can read. Use it to create a "Reading Success" bulletin board or a class book.

- *Value student writing.* Celebrate student attempts at writing—from scribbling and drawing to invented spelling and conventional writing. Focus on what students *can* do.
- *Encourage frequent and varied writing.* Writing across the curriculum should be a daily occurrence. Students can label, list, caption, describe, document, and create in print.
- *Provide a classroom environment rich in print, literature, and language.* Fill the classroom with student work, environmental print, charts, and books. Encourage students to use language in all of its domains.

A Writing Development Case Study

The following case study tracks the progress of one English learner from Vietnam.

Linh, was born in Vietnam and spoke Chinese at home. When she was 5, she arrived in Canada, and although her father was a teacher in schools in Vietnam, Linh did not attend kindergarten. In September of the following year, Linh at age 5.9 was placed in a first-grade classroom. At the time, she was able to speak a few words and simple phrases in English. During the year that the following samples were written, she received half-hour daily instruction in English.

In Linh's writing samples we can see how she grappled with the various aspects of writing: creating ideas, symbolic representation, spelling, and the conventions of English grammar, punctuation, and capitalization.

The case study and its illustrations are reprinted from *Whole Language Strategies for ESL Students* by Gail Heald-Taylor, © 1997. Reprinted with the permission of University of Toronto Press.

Linh: Sept. 12, 1983. Age 5.9

1 **First Grade, September:** In the fall, Linh used scribbles to symbolically represent the stories she wrote. Her first scribble had a strong resemblance to Chinese characters, the print she would likely see in her home.

I walking with my friend to play with her. I play the teacher. It fun to play. and my friend. I'm the teacher. my is a kid.
Linh Oct. 6, 1983. Age 5.10

2 **First Grade, October:** Linh's horizontal scribble, written in a left-to-right motion across the page to describe playing with her friend, indicates that she is aware of the direction of English print.

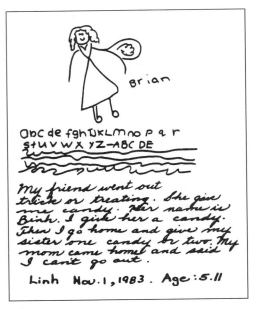

Linh Nov. 1, 1983. Age: 5.11

3 **First Grade, Beginning of November:** In this sample, Linh has used conventional alphabet letters as well as scribbles to symbolically represent her story about Halloween. Although she was aware that conventional letters are used in text, she doesn't know how to use them appropriately.

rain-day

Linh Nov. 15, 1983. Age: 5.11

4 **First Grade, Mid-November:** In this rain story, Linh has represented the text with scribble symbols except for the word *rain-day,* which she read and copied from a group chart. It is interesting that in her "reading," *rain-day* was not included as part of the oral translation.

My mom make me a cookie.

Linh: Dec. 1983. Age: 6.0

5 **First Grade, December:** By December, Linh had begun to read and included the sight vocabulary she knew in her composition (*my, mom, a, I, am*). She was also aware of sound-symbol relationships and used this knowledge in her consonant spellings (*m_____* for *made, c_____* for *cookie*).

It is fun to go to skating because it's fun. I like to go skating.

Linh: Jan. 5, 1984. Age: 6.1

6 **First Grade, Beginning of January:** Linh spelled most words accurately in this story and used scribbles only as placeholders for parts of words she couldn't spell.

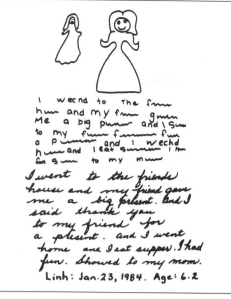

7 **First Grade, Mid-January:** In this sample, Linh has concentrated on developing the composition. Her story about receiving a present from a friend contains five complete thoughts about a single topic. She uses many correct spellings, numerous consonant spellings, and relies on scribbles as placeholders for the unknown orthography.

8 **First Grade, End of January:** By the end of January, Linh represented her stories with only conventional symbols and ceased to scribble.

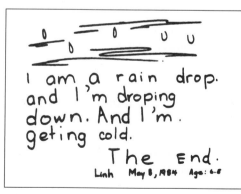

9 **First Grade, May:** During the spring, Linh appeared to be concentrating on spelling, grammar, and punctuation rather than on composition. In this May sample, she has spelled most words correctly, has learned rules of grammar (*droping, geting*), and has begun to use the period appropriately.

10 **Second Grade, September:** In September, Linh again focused on developing the composition, and although the stories lengthened and the spelling had stabilized, there was no evidence of punctuation.

> Once a upon a time there were a farm. And they are eating lunch. And then the two children went outside to play. And one of the children open the door of the cow's door. And then they went inside. And then when the door was still open. And then the cows went out. And then the little children went out to play again. And then they saw the cow was gone. And then they run. And go find the cow. And then they went to the woods. And then they hear a sound like a cow. And then they went into the woods And then they found the cows. And they went out of the woods. And then they saw someone with a light. And it was the children's mother. And then they went home.
>
> Linh Nov. 6, 1984. Age: 6.11

11 **Second Grade, November:** By November, Linh had begun to truly integrate the conventions of writing including symbolic representation, spelling, and composition.

RESPONDING TO LITERATURE

Providing rich and varied ways for students to respond to literature leads to deeper understanding and comprehension. As students respond, they analyze and then internalize story structure and key literary elements such as character, setting, sequence, voice, and perspective. They play with the writing of others—practicing it, changing it here and there—and begin to make the elements, structures, and devices their own. The following are examples of ways students can respond to literature and expand their own command of language and literacy.

Re-Creations

Re-creations are student-produced pieces of writing that reproduce the exact text of a literature selection. Reproduced stories use the language of the original story, with students providing their own illustrations. Reproductions allow students to internalize the language of the selection and extend it in artistic or symbolic ways. The language remains understandable and readable.

Innovations

Innovations are writings that are both inspired by and maintain the basic structure, pattern, rhythm, or topic of a selection, but give it a new twist. Students may change any element of the story, poem, or song to make it their own. For example, students may make innovations titled *Take Me Out to the Shopping Mall/Soccerfield* or *The Twelve Days of Camping*. Innovations provide rich opportunities for language and concept expansion. In addition, cueing systems are utilized and developed within meaningful contexts.

TIP Use re-creations as an art lesson to replicate the artistic style or techniques of an illustrator. For example, use collage with stories by Eric Carle or Leo Lionni and pencil drawings for Chris Van Allsburg, Maurice Sendak, or Shel Silverstein.

Use the Literary Innovations template on page 133 of the Resource Pages to brainstorm ideas for new content, titles, story lines, and characters for a favorite literary selection.

Story Mapping

Story mapping can take several forms. In each case, significant elements of stories are identified and organized in a visual format. Story maps range from literal illustrations or descriptions of important elements to symbolic representations of these elements. Story maps may be completed individually, with partners, or in collaborative groups. It is always interesting to see how individuals or groups interpret and represent the same story.

Story Reporting Map

These story maps include specific bits of information that students must identify or report about the story. Typical elements might include characters, setting, problem, sequence, and solution.

STORY REPORTING MAP ●

STORY TITLE		
Characters	Setting	Problem
Beginning	Middle	End

Simple Retelling

Simple retellings involve students in identifying and illustrating the five to seven major events in a story. The illustrations are matched to text (summaries of the events) and compiled in a book or wall story. Guide students in identifying the sequence by first identifying beginning, middle, and end. Next ask what happened between the beginning and the middle and between the middle and the end for five events.

SIMPLE RETELLING MAP ●

EVENT 1 (Illustration)	EVENT 2	EVENT 3	EVENT 4	EVENT 5
Description of the event goes here . . .	Description of the event goes here . . .	Description of the event goes here . . .	Description of the event goes here . . .	Description of the event goes here . . .

> **TIP** Story mapping serves to develop deeper, less tangible literacy skills, such as an understanding of plot, characterization, imagery, allusion, and perspective.

Excitement Map

Excitement maps are extensions of a simple retelling. Students first illustrate, on small pieces of paper, the events of the simple retelling. Next, on chart paper, they draw a graph. The events are written sequentially along the horizontal axis. The vertical column is numbered 1–10. Students select the most exciting part of the story and place it above the matching text at the 10 at the top of the chart. They continue ranking the remaining events accordingly. The completed map visually demonstrates the building excitement and climax of the story. (*Note:* Individuals or groups may map their stories differently. Encourage them to justify their work.)

EXCITEMENT MAP

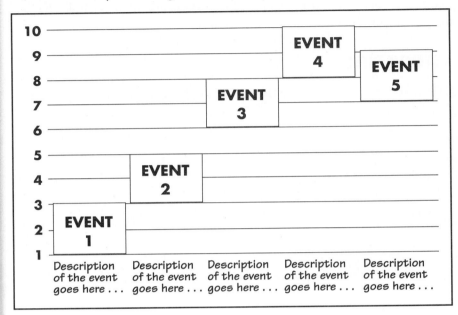

Actual Map

Actual maps are story maps that identify and locate the various places that make up the setting or settings of a story. Students illustrate the beginning and continue by drawing a path leading to other places where the action occurred. The events are connected by the path. The direction and shape of the path are determined by the students. Students then add details, such as characters and significant items, and label the items on the map.[56]

ACTUAL MAP

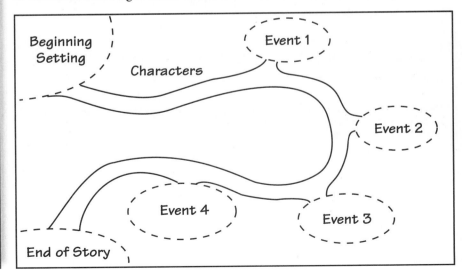

Symbolic Map

Symbolic maps use symbols and illustrations to represent the significant elements of a story. Words are used not to label but to symbolize or represent ideas. Students represent the key elements of the story in such a way that they can be used to retell the story. An example of a symbolic map for The Boy Who Cried Wolf appears below.

Chapter 4 identifies and describes additional graphic organizers that can be used to develop literature and literacy.

SYMBOLIC MAP

Refer to and review the Preview page for this chapter (page 47). Was your prior knowledge accurate? (Did you have any misconceptions or inaccurate ideas?)

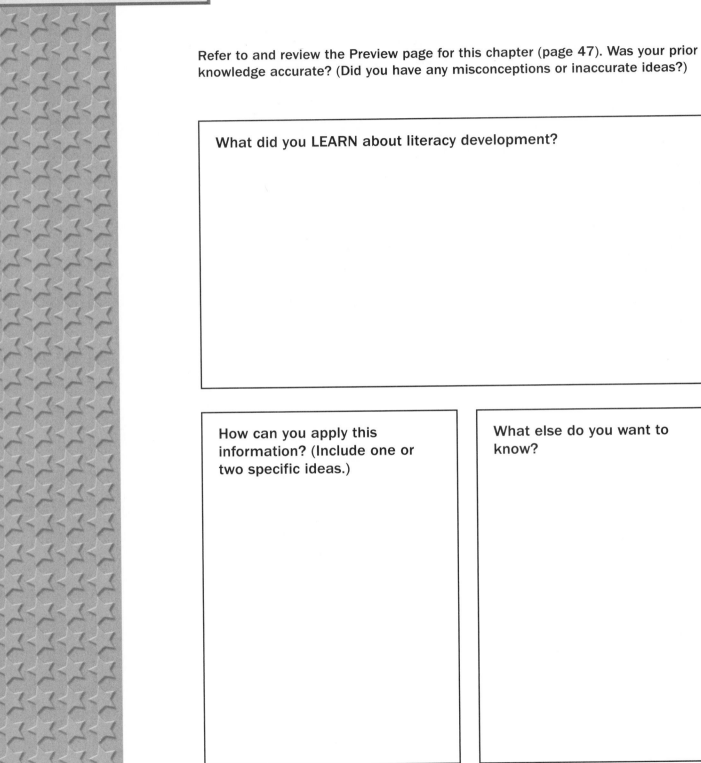

What did you LEARN about literacy development?

How can you apply this information? (Include one or two specific ideas.)

What else do you want to know?

Academic/ Content Area Development

> From a pedagogical point of view, the integration of language and academic instruction means that mastery of academic skills and information provides a natural basis for second language teaching and learning. It is based on the intellectual skills and knowledge considered important for communicating about and understanding the academic subject matter set out in the program of instruction. Proficiency in the target language is not seen as a prerequisite to academic development but rather as a co-requisite. It is a means to an end.
>
> —Fred Genesee, *Integrating Language and Content*[1]

It has been noted that we—as educators—require something of all English learners that is not required or even expected of native-English speakers; that is, we require English learners to learn enough of a second language to be able to function and do high-level academic work in the new language. Further, the expectation for virtually all English learners is that this goal be reached in a relatively short period of time.

The task is daunting. It is clear that English learners must acquire high levels of English in addition to developing the academic knowledge and skills that will enable them to succeed in school. This chapter focuses on how to provide access to and further develop the academic or content area curriculum for students who are also learning English, the language of instruction.

What do you already KNOW about academic/content area development?

What do you WANT to know or learn?

FOCUSING ON THE LEARNER

Students come to our classes with varied backgrounds, cultures, languages, and ways of learning. All instruction begins with the student. The needs of the student determine the starting point and the strategies and approaches that will best promote learning across the curriculum. Using this *student-centered approach,* teachers should consider many factors in determining how students learn best and then apply this information to classroom practices.

ACCESSING CORE CURRICULUM: PROMISING PRACTICES

A basic right of all students in United States is to have access to grade-level-appropriate content instruction. This right has been affirmed through the courts, is embedded in civil rights law, and most recently was reaffirmed by the sweeping "No Child Left Behind" federal legislation. The intent of the law is clearly to provide access to core curriculum to *all students*—meaning *every single one.* Accomplishing this goal presents unique challenges for English learners who are taught primarily through English—a language in which they are not yet fully proficient. To achieve this goal, it is important to provide academic core curriculum instruction to English learners in ways that will enable them to understand concepts and content. This chapter describes specific strategies for providing such instruction, including using temporary supports, or "scaffolds," and Specially Designed Academic Instruction in English (SDAIE).

> *Effective instruction for immigrant students should be guided by (1) high standards for learning, (2) a belief that second language learners can achieve them, and (3) knowledge of how to structure teaching and learning to support students in their gradual acquisition of sophisticated proficiencies.*
>
> —Aida Walqui, *Access and Engagement*[2]

The content area approaches and strategies presented in the following sections will assist teachers in identifying and then providing the special support (or "help") that will promote English learners' access to grade-level content at increasingly higher levels.

Teaching Within the Zone

> *You use the voices of others to guide you . . . until you can use your own voice as the guide.*
>
> —Aida Walqui[3]

A fundamental principle that describes how students learn and thereby shapes instructional practice is the construct of teaching within the "zone of proximal development." The idea of scaffolding instruction is supported by Vygotsky's idea of focusing instruction at a level that is just beyond students' independent ability level but not so far off that learning is unattainable.[4] This "zone of proximal development" as Vygotsky calls it, is the students' instructional level, or the level at which students can function with the help of specific instructional supports and guidance. It is within this instructional range, or "zone of understanding," that teachers should focus

Remember how hard your first day of algebra seemed? You barely understood, but were able to do the work with help from the teacher. That night, however, you struggled to understand and do your homework independently.

The classroom instruction was within your zone ("with help") but you were not yet able to work independently (beyond the zone). By the end of the semester, as you looked back, that first day's work appeared easy (independent or "known").

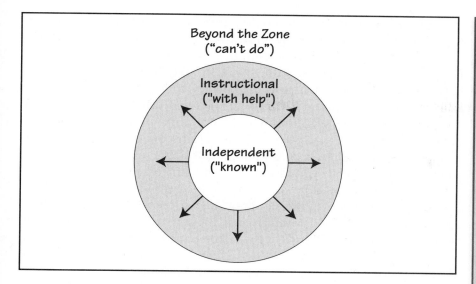

Beyond the Zone
("can't do")

Instructional
("with help")

Independent
("known")

TEACHING AND LEARNING ZONES

Good teachers, then, teach just beyond what
students already know.

their attention in providing instruction that will move students forward in learning and conceptual development. Instruction is just far enough ahead of students' conceptual and linguistic development to stretch their levels of competence, but not so far ahead that it is frustrating and ineffective.[5] As Aida Walqui said of learning within the zone of proximal development, "You use the voices of others to guide you until you can use your own voice as the guide."[6]

The zone of proximal development is a concept that is fundamental to our understanding of how students learn. In Chapter 3, the related concept of the "gradual release of responsibility" is presented as a principle for literacy instruction. The zone of proximal development is the theoretical basis for instruction **to, with,** and **by** students.

Refer to Chapter 3, page 50, for information on the gradual release of responsibility.

Specially Designed Academic Instruction in English (SDAIE)

Involve students in complex, compelling tasks that engage them in intellectual challenges. AMPLIFY, DON'T SIMPLIFY.

—Aida Walqui, *Academic Language*[7]

Specially Designed Academic Instruction in English (SDAIE), also referred to as Sheltered English, is instruction that is provided in English and combines the principles of second language acquisition with elements of good teaching that make the content comprehensible to students.[8] SDAIE has emerged as a "collective" response to teaching core curriculum in English to students who are not yet fully proficient in English. It is not a single approach but rather a collection of highly effective instructional strategies aimed at making content understandable and accessible to English learners. SDAIE involves the careful selection of materials and resources as well as the skillful application of teaching strategies and techniques that provide access to content by all students.

English learners face a double challenge: they must simultaneously learn core curriculum (through English) and they must learn English. The central goal of SDAIE is to provide access to grade-level content-related curriculum. Along with this, however, SDAIE also serves to further develop English language proficiency (particularly academic language proficiency), higher-level thinking skills, and advanced literacy skills.[9]

Learning and comprehension are often a matter of degree; we begin with simple understandings that grow and take shape with each opportunity to learn and practice. Eventually, these shades of meaning coalesce to form deep understandings. Rather than simplify language and complex ideas, teachers should, therefore, *amplify* key concepts, with many more examples that are given in a variety of ways and using varying forms of language. This language redundancy, common in authentic language exchanges, supports comprehension and learning. SDAIE provides for this natural language redundancy with abundant opportunities to learn, use, and practice both language and content in meaningful contexts.

Effective SDAIE must be very clear and focused. Teachers will continually build "scaffolds of understanding" and support as the needs arise. Teachers utilizing SDAIE, therefore, may not cover all topics in great depth but instead will identify and focus on key understandings and concepts that are crucial to students' understanding. Daily instructional activities must link back to the key ideas and concepts until they are firmly understood. Core concepts are developed by redistributing materials and identifying areas of potential emphasis, resulting in a greater depth of learning. As Aida Walqui writes, "We may have *covered* less, but in the end, we will have *uncovered* more."[10]

SDAIE has often been referred to as *just good teaching*. While this is true, in that good teaching matches skillful instruction to the specific needs of students, SDAIE strategies such as those presented here are *essential* to the academic success of English learners.

Scaffolds: Scaffolding Instruction

Scaffolds are temporary structures, strategies, or aids that teachers use to enable students to build their own understanding. Scaffolds include visual or auditory supports that enable students to participate in knowledge acquisition and problem-solving activities from the very beginning. Supported by effective scaffolding, students are able to develop an understanding that would otherwise be beyond their reach.[11] Aida Walqui identifies and describes the following scaffolds for supporting English learners in accessing the core curriculum.[12]

Modeling
Modeling, or demonstrating, provides students with a clear picture of what is expected. The extralinguistic clues clarify directions and provide concrete examples of the finished product. Any task that is introduced for the first time should be modeled.

Bridging
Bridging involves activating prior knowledge to establish a connection to new information. Tapping into prior knowledge or experience provides a personal link that demonstrates the relevance of the new material to students' lives, linking the known to the unknown. Bridging is accomplished in a variety of ways including brainstorming, developing anticipatory charts (graphic organizers), and identifying related literature, resources, or experiences.

Note: SDAIE instruction also involves the use of language acquisition strategies. Refer to Chapter 2 for such strategies, including "Techniques for Providing Comprehensible Input" on page 33.

Identify ways in which you have used or can use the following scaffolds to help students access core curriculum.

Contextualization

Teachers cannot rely on words alone to convey meaning, particularly to those not yet proficient in the language. Words must be embedded in context to make the meaning clear. It is this context that helps students construct the meaning of largely unfamiliar words. Using visuals, manipulatives, video clips, graphic organizers, and other realia (real stuff!) serves to contextualize language and thereby promote understanding. The entire classroom should be considered a learning tool that can be used to bring context and comprehension to the learning experience.

Schema Building

Schema building involves bringing to light the connections that exist between and across concepts and the curriculum. Students may not automatically make these connections. Using strategies such as advance organizers, graphic organizers, story mapping, and jigsaw projects, students gain a wider perspective on how concepts fit together and how they may fit in the larger scheme of things.

Metacognitive Development

Metacognitive development involves the explicit teaching and learning of strategies that enable students to become autonomous learners. This conscious development of strategies and skills enables students to tackle academic tasks at increasingly higher levels. The Cognitive Academic Language Learning Approach (CALLA), reciprocal teaching, K-W-L-H activities (What I KNOW, What I WANT to Know, What I LEARNED, HOW I Learned), think alouds, and directed reading-thinking are examples of such strategies.

Text Re-presentation

Text re-presentation involves taking a known (previously read) text and manipulating it for a new purpose, for instance, summarizing a story or chapter, writing captions in order to capture the main ideas, writing an "eye-witness" account of a historical event, changing a narrative into a dialog (or vice versa), writing a play or reader's theater based on a text, or developing collaborative posters or dialogs. Text re-presentation requires in-depth comprehension of a text, and it also allows students to use a familiar text to practice and extend writing (reading and speaking) to a new genre and for a new purpose.

Language in Content Instruction: Challenges and Supports

Active Engagement

To actively engage in classroom activities, students must possess the language structures that enable them to participate. For example, students must know how to agree or disagree, express an opinion, or ask for clarification. What often prevents engagement is simply the inability to begin the sentence in English.

This difficulty is particularly prevalent in academic settings where students are expected to use a "public voice." Engaging in a group discussion usually requires a more formal, or academic, form of English. Students may need instruction and guidance in appropriately applying this form (register) of English.

Refer to page 96 for some of the language structures that students should have at their command.

Refer to Chapter 2, page 20, for more information on language register.

LANGUAGE STRUCTURES FOR ACTIVE ENGAGEMENT

Acknowledging Ideas

Agreeing/Disagreeing
- *I agree/don't agree with _____ because . . .*
- *I think/don't think _____ is right because . . .*
- *I got the same/different answer.*

Affirming
- *That's an interesting way to think of it.*
- *I see what you mean.*
- *I hadn't thought of that.*

Relating
- *My idea is similar to . . .*
- *That reminds me of . . .*

Rephrasing
- *You're saying that . . .*
- *In other words, . . .*
- *What I'm hearing you say is . . .*

Expressing Opinions
- *I think/believe/imagine that . . .*
- *In my opinion . . .*

Asking for Clarification
- *Could you say that again?*
- *What did you mean?*
- *I still have a question about . . .*
- *Did you mean . . .*

Individual/Group Reporting
- *I/We learned/discovered/found out that . . .*
- *_____ showed me that . . .*
- *I/We agreed/didn't agree that . . .*

Holding the Floor
- *As I was saying, . . .*
- *What I was trying to say . . .*
- *If I could finish . . .*
- *Let me finish.*

—Adapted from Kate Kinsella, *Expository Writing Scaffolds for English Learners in Content Area Classrooms.* California Department of Education, Santa Barbara, CA, 2001a. Used with permission of the author.

Understanding the Task

Students are constantly given tasks that require them to process and/or present information in specific ways. For example, students might be asked to do any of the following related to a specific concept:

- *Define* photosynthesis.
- *Describe* photosynthesis.
- *Diagram* photosynthesis.

To successfully complete each task, students must understand *what is being asked* and *what specific information is required* to complete the task. Describing *photosynthesis* is not the same as defining it. Students must first be able to distinguish the demands of the task before they can be expected to successfully complete it.

Kate Kinsella has identified the following tasks that are frequently given in academic reading and writing assignments.[13]

Analyze:	Break a subject down into parts and explain the parts.
Compare:	Show how things are similar and different.
Contrast:	Show how things are different.
Critique:	Point out good and bad points.
Define:	Give an accurate meaning with sufficient detail.
Describe:	Include sufficient detail so that the topic or subject can be visualized and/or understood.
Diagram:	Make a drawing of something and label its parts.
Discuss:	Give a complete and detailed answer, including key points.
Enumerate:	Count off or list examples, reasons, or effects.
Evaluate:	Give an opinion of the value of something, based on good/bad points, strengths/weaknesses, and so on.
Explain:	Give the meaning of something, providing facts and details that make it understood.
Illustrate:	Clarify a point or idea by giving examples.

Instructional Materials

How to Select

Learning grade-level core curriculum is the primary goal of SDAIE. This does not mean, however, that the same materials must be used to accomplish this goal. English learners benefit most from materials that provide extra clues to meaning through appropriate and abundant visuals, diagrams, and text supports, such as captions and labels. Criteria for selection should include the following:

- *Comprehensibility:* Are the materials comprehensible to English learners? Do consistent devices support and enhance comprehension? Is the text itself structured and formatted clearly and consistently?

- *Quality content:* Does the content meet the course objectives and grade-level standards for the subject? Is it up to date and of the same high quality required for all students?

- *Appeal:* Does the material appeal to the ages and interests of the students? Will it appeal to a variety of learning styles? Is the material visually appealing?

Review the materials you use for one content area, then answer the following questions:

- How do you supplement to promote meaning and provide extra clues for English learners?

- How do your materials rate in terms of comprehensibility, quality, and appeal?

Refer to Chapter 3, page 64, for more information on selecting texts for English learners.

Cracking the Text Code

Large textbooks can seem overwhelming to English learners. Support students in accessing these texts by helping them crack the textbook code.

- Show students how to use a book's navigation aids, such as the table of contents, glossary, or index.
- Study the format of each chapter and section. Explain the purpose of study guides, headings, highlighted vocabulary terms, illustration captions, and review questions.
- Help students preview a section of text to determine what it is about and how they can identify and locate key information quickly.
- Discuss how information is organized in the text or in a specific chapter: chronolologically, topically, following a cause-effect or compare-contrast pattern, and so on. Discuss how recognizing this organizational structure can help students better process and understand the information presented. Prepare students by pointing out examples and explaining, *This is how it looks and this is how you approach and read this kind of text.*

Modifying the Text

How have you successfully modified content material for English learners?

The language and reading level of core curriculum textbooks is often beyond the linguistic abilities of English learners. It is therefore likely that many materials will need some modification to make them accessible to students of English. In modifying a text, the goal is to increase comprehensibility without watering down the content. There are many ways to do this.

Use excerpts: Rather than assigning students an entire section of text to read, identify and use an important excerpt. Paraphrase the content (or story line) leading up to the selected excerpt to create context. Then have students read the excerpt and discuss what they have learned. This technique provides students with a greater exposure to a variety of texts and content and allows the teacher to focus on the most significant aspects of the text or learning.

Read to and with students: Read sections aloud to students, or utilize the shared reading approach by having students read the text with you. Paraphrase, pause to clarify, and point out challenging content or language elements in the text. You may also have students read along with tape-recorded segments of text.

Simplify, expand, or define key concepts or vocabulary: It is frequently necessary to develop the key concepts or vocabulary as the teacher is reading to or with students. Richard-Amato and Snow demonstrate how the techniques of simplification, expansion, and direct definition can be used to quickly aid comprehension of the sentence, *The government's funds were depleted.*[14]

- *Simplification:* The government's funds were depleted. The government was almost out of money.
- *Expansion of ideas:* The government's funds were depleted. The government had spent a lot of money on many things: guns, equipment, help for the poor. It did not have any more money to spend on anything else.
- *Direct definition:* The government's funds were depleted. This means that the government had spent all its money.

Teach language patterns and structures: Texts, particularly nonfiction materials, frequently utilize consistent language structures to bring order and sequence to the text. Assist students in identifying and using features such as the following:

- Paragraphs that begin with the main idea followed by supporting details
- Use of linguistic markers or signal words, such as *first, next, then* to indicate sequence; *because* to indicate cause and effect; *but* or *however* to indicate contrast

Refer to Chapter 3, page 70, for a list of additional signal words.

Rewrite/reconfigure text: There are many ways in which the text itself can be reconfigured to make it more comprehensible.

- Rewrite excerpts or paragraphs so that they contain key information in a consistent format, or use key signal words such as those listed previously.
- Use portions of text rewritten by English-speaking students.
- Use advanced and graphic organizers to represent key information visually.
- Use the scaffold "text re-presentation" to represent text in a different way.

Refer to pages 106 and 107 for more information on graphic organizers.

Refer to "Scaffolds: Scaffolding Instruction" on page 94.

Supplement the text: Supplement the textbook with support materials that enhance language and concept development, such as maps, visuals of all sorts, newspaper and magazine articles, graphic organizers and reference charts, videos/DVDs, audio tapes/CDs, computer programs, the Internet, and other interactive technologies.

The modifications described increase comprehensibility and readability. As student proficiency increases, so does the complexity of the reading. The goal of modifying texts is to ensure access to core curriculum while building in students the academic strength, skills, and flexibility needed to be able to work with texts that are not modified.

The Cognitive Academic Language Learning Approach (CALLA)

The Cognitive Academic Language Learning Approach (CALLA) is a strategy that intentionally moves students beyond conversational language fluency (BICS) and promotes the acquisition of *academic* language *proficiency* (CALP). It has long been noted that many English learners who appear quite fluent in English still require additional assistance in achieving *academic success* in English. CALLA is an approach that focuses *explicitly* on teaching students strategies that they can apply to their own learning so that they will become autonomous learners. These strategies empower students to achieve academically. CALLA integrates:

Refer to Chapter 2, page 21, for a review of BICS and CALP.

- *Content:* Key concepts and ideas from core curriculum
- *Language:* The language needed to access the content
- *Strategies:* The special techniques students apply and use on their own to help them learn

The focus on explicit development of academic learning strategies combined with language learning is unique to CALLA.

The CALLA model for academic language learning was originally developed by Anna Uhl Chamot and J. Michael O'Malley.

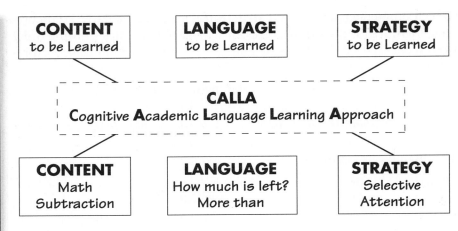

Review the CALLA strategies on page 101. Identify the strategies you use to

- Plan a lesson
- Plan a vacation/trip
- Learn the lyrics of a song

Anna Uhl Chamot and J. Michael O'Malley surveyed students from various language backgrounds to determine what they did that enabled them to achieve academically. They found that these achievers utilized strategies that helped them learn in school. Chamot and O'Malley classified the strategies under three headings:

- Metacognitive strategies
- Cognitive strategies
- Social affective strategies

Metacognitive strategies help students think about, plan, monitor, and evaluate learning. *Cognitive strategies* help students as they are engaged in the learning process. They involve interacting with and/or manipulating the material mentally or physically, and applying a specific technique to the learning task. *Social affective strategies* help students interact with another person, accomplish a task, or obtain assistance in learning.

Chamot and O'Malley realized that these strategies could be explicitly taught. Once students have a working knowledge of each strategy, they can employ them at will as the need arises. The teaching of these learning strategies became the framework for CALLA.[15]

Page 101 lists and briefly describes each strategy. CALLA serves as a powerful tool for moving students at high levels of English language proficiency toward full cognitive academic language proficiency and academic success.

BRAINSTORM
What are the three strategies you think your students should know immediately? Why?

CALLA LEARNING STRATEGIES

Metacognitive Strategies

Advance Organization
Previewing the main ideas and concepts of the material to be learned, often by skimming the text for the organizing principle

Advance Preparation
Rehearsing the language needed for an oral or written task

Organizational Planning
Planning the parts, sequence, and main ideas to be expressed orally or in writing

Selective Attention
Attending to, or scanning, key words, phrases, linguistic markers, sentences, or types of information

Self-Evaluation
Judging how well one has accomplished a learning activity after it has been completed

Cognitive Strategies

Contextualization
Placing a word or phrase in a meaningful sentence or category

Elaboration
Relating new information to what is already known

Grouping
Classifying words, terminology, or concepts according to their attributes

Imagery
Using visual images (either mental or actual) to understand and remember new information

Inferencing
Using information in the text to guess meanings of new items, predict outcomes, or complete missing parts

Note-Taking
Writing down key words and concepts in abbreviated form while listening or reading

Resourcing
Using reference materials such as dictionaries, encyclopedias, or textbooks

Summarizing
Making a mental or written summary of information gained from listening or reading

Transfer
Using what is already known to facilitate a learning task

Social Affective Strategies

Cooperation
Working together with peers to solve a problem, pool information, check a learning task, or get feedback on oral or written performance

Questioning for Clarification
Eliciting from a teacher or peer additional explanation, rephrasing, or examples

Self-Talk
Reducing anxiety by using mental techniques that make one feel competent to do the learning task

From *The CALLA Handbook: Implementing the Cognitive Academic Language Learning Approach* by Anna Uhl Chamot and J. Michael O'Malley, © 1994. Reprinted by permission of Addison-Wesley Publishing Company.

Cooperative/Collaborative Learning

Cooperative learning . . . structures talk around content, requiring that students develop improved skills in thinking, and in language, in order to explain, persuade, encourage, disagree, inform, discuss, and negotiate. It provides ideal opportunities for second-language learners to hear and practice English beyond social language.

—Mary Meyers, *Teaching to Diversity*[16]

Cooperative and collaborative learning requires students to interact and rely on others and themselves to accomplish a task. These interactions may be structured formally, with each student being assigned a specific and defined role in the group, or informally, with students collaborating to accomplish the task. When small groups of students collaborate on a common task, they must clarify and negotiate meaning with one another. This interactive exchange of information and ideas provides a rich language-learning opportunity for English learners.

The cooperative learning environment offers many other rewards. Learners become more active, self-directed, and communicative. Academic achievement as well as discipline often improve as students experience success and take an active interest in what they are doing.

In addition, many English language learners come from home cultures that value cooperation, sharing, and group achievement. A cooperative classroom is a particularly affirming environment for these students.

Many resources are available to help teachers fully utilize cooperative learning in all subject areas.[17] Mary Meyers identifies four major principles of cooperative learning:[18]

1. Cooperative tasks are structured so that no one individual can complete the learning task alone.
2. Positive interdependence is fostered and developed. Students are evaluated individually and as a group.
3. Students work in different teams. Teams can be of three types: interest groups, random selection, or heterogeneous teams. The team configuration depends on the complexity, duration, and purpose of the task. Students are given opportunities to participate in a variety of groups.
4. Students learn both social and language skills necessary for cooperation at the same time as they learn content/concepts.

The following cooperative learning strategies or structures are particularly helpful with English learners.

Brainstorming

Brainstorming can be accomplished with the whole class or a small group. The key is that all ideas are valid and recorded. Information from brainstorming can later be organized and categorized for easy use and retrieval.

Think-Pair-Share

This strategy has three components.

- *Think:* Students think carefully about the question (and answer).
- *Pair:* Each student finds a partner.
- *Share:* Partners share answers and prepare to share both answers with the entire class.

TIP This type of interactive learning is particularly helpful for English learners because it provides meaningful opportunities to use English in varied contexts with varied English speakers for varied purposes.

TIP It is helpful to post the procedures for common structures on chart paper so that groups can refer to the process as they work.

TIP Have students jot down or sketch their answers. This forces them to be accountable for participation.

Numbered Heads

Students work in groups of four.

- Students number themselves from 1 to 4.
- The teacher asks a discussion question.
- Each group discusses the question and develops a team answer. Each member of the team must be able to answer the question.
- The teacher calls a number. The member from each team with the corresponding number raises a hand to respond. The teacher selects one "number X" to respond.

Novel Ideas

Novel ideas is used in conjunction with other structures. It may be used with partners or small groups.

- Students brainstorm and list ideas or answers to a question.
- Groups take turns sharing their list. Each group may name only the ideas or answers that have not previously been mentioned.
- Students must listen attentively and eliminate common answers from their lists, responding with *novel ideas only*.

Round-Robin

The round-robin strategy has students take turns sharing their ideas, giving answers, or adding information. No one interrupts. All have a turn.

Jigsaw

Also called expert groups, jigsaw is a four-step structure.

- Students form a "home" group of three to five.
- Students number off. Each member is responsible for mastering one part of the assignment.
- Students move to form an "expert" group with students from other groups with the same number (for example, all 1s, all 2s, and so on). This expert group completes their assigned part of the task, and each of its members is capable of teaching the information.
- Students return to their home groups. Each expert shares (or teaches) the content learned in the expert group with the members of the home group.

Environmental Supports

The classroom itself should support English learners in developing language and academic knowledge. To become a supportive learning environment, the classroom should provide the following:

- Organized resources should be available, such as wall space dedicated to literacy, math, and so on; clearly labeled classroom libraries; and accessible reference materials. Students know where to look or go for specific types of support.
- Resources that help organize language and learning, such as word walls or graphic organizers, and relevant charts should be accessible.
- The classroom should be student centered. Students see themselves and their learning in the environment and are able to use the room to reflect on and extend their own learning.

TIP Organize a schematic word wall in which words and phrases are organized around a specific content area topic.

- Plenty of visuals should clarify language and meaning.
- The room should be appealing. It should be attractive with a sense of order that supports and motivates students.
- The classroom must be used. Post only the supports students need and use.

Charting Student Learning

The process of charting is an instructional tool that shapes the learning experience and helps to organize and clarify thinking, language, and connections. Charting student learning creates a resource students can refer to during independent work; it also provides a record of learning. The added dimension of *order* is brought to language and concepts and helps to clarify language and learning. *Charts should be co-constructed with students* to help students process information and construct meaning.

In the chart below, students read a simple text that includes language patterns usually reserved for books, not common in everyday speech. The teacher charts the written and spoken language to demonstrate the differences in the way language is used in speech and in books. This type of chart is used to clarify and extend meaning. Students watch and listen for additional examples to add to the chart and also use the chart as a reference. (For example, students might refer to the chart when creating a story innovation using natural speech.)

Instructional charts like the ones on this page can be used to help students process information and construct meaning.

Book Talk	Everyday Talk
· *Away went the darkness.*	· *The darkness went away.*
· *Away went all my fear.*	· *All my fear went away.*
· *Happy became my heart.*	· *My heart became happy.*

In the example below, students explore the sound/spelling relationship between verbs ending in -*ed*. Students analyze the chart to identify patterns and trends that can enhance reading and writing. Students add words to the chart as they are encountered and refer to the chart to support writing.

All About -*ed*		
t **sound**	*d* **sound**	*ed* **sound**
jump**ed**	play**ed**	add**ed**
fish**ed**	yell**ed**	land**ed**
walk**ed**	grabb**ed**	melt**ed**
dress**ed**	pil**ed**	need**ed**

Keep current! Use your valuable wall space wisely.

Once students have fully internalized the concept and no longer need the visual support, remove the chart. Display only the charts that are in active use.

Strategies We Know

To keep the learning environment current and to reinforce what students are learning, post a chart labeled "Strategies We Know." When a previously charted strategy is fully understood and no longer needed by students, transfer the strategy name or title to the "Strategies We Know" chart. Students may still refer to this chart to remind them to apply these known strategies. The chart also provides a record of student learning.

Graphic Organizers

Graphic organizers are tools that help to visually organize information. They are useful across the curriculum, from developing basic vocabulary to identifying and synthesizing elements of literature and processing information in core content areas.

Advance organizers, also known as "anticipatory guides," are graphic organizers used to begin a new unit of study. They serve to identify what students already know about a topic and also to create a context for learning more. K-W-L-H charts are familiar forms of advance organizers. Another type asks students to predict answers to questions around the unit of study. Students provide a rationale for their predictions and revisit the chart when the unit is completed.

There is some evidence to show that graphic organizers actually help the brain to store and process information more efficiently. Graphic organizers are particularly useful in aiding comprehension for English learners as they visually represent, organize, and contextualize language.

TIP Add drama to the process. After reviewing the "known" chart and adding its title to the "Strategies We Know" chart, tell students, *Well, you don't need this chart any more because now it is in your heads!* Then rip the chart into pieces and throw it away!

Refer to page 106 for varied examples of graphic organizers. See page 107 for ways to use graphic organizers in content areas.

GRAPHIC ORGANIZERS
EXAMPLES AND APPLICATIONS

K-W-L-H

K	W	L	H
What I KNOW	What I WANT to know	What I LEARNED	HOW I learned

Background Knowledge/Evaluate Learning

VENN DIAGRAM

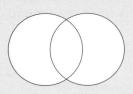

Comparing/Contrasting

ANTICIPATORY/INPUT CHART

True	False	Statement

Background/Prior Knowledge

CLUSTER

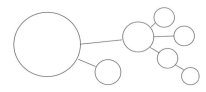

Brainstorming/Organizing Information

WEB

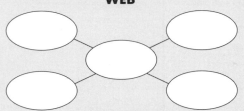

Analyzing Attributes/Words

T-CHART

Looks Like	Sounds Like

Visualizing/Comparing Attributes

PICTORIAL INPUT

Building Vocabulary and Background

DESCRIPTIVE WEB

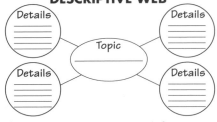

Organizing Key/Supportive Information

MATRIX/PROCESS GRID

Animal	Body Covering	Backbone
snake		
dog		

Classifying/Comparing Information

SEQUENCE-OF-EVENTS CHAIN

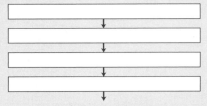

Visually Sequencing Events

Venn Diagram: Social Studies

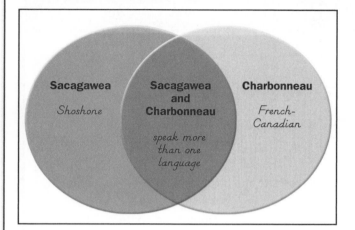

Process Grid: Science/Language Arts (Greek and Latin Roots)

Greek or Latin Root	Greek or Latin Word	New Word
carn- (flesh; meat)	*vorare* (to eat)	**carnivore**
herba- (plant)	*vorare* (to eat)	**herbivore**
omni- (everything)	*vorare* (to eat)	**omnivore**
inter- (between; together)	*actus* (to do)	**interact**
organ- (tool; part of the body; activity)	*-ism* (condition of)	**organism**
eco- (house; natural environment)	*systema* (placing together)	**ecosystem**

Word Web: Social Studies

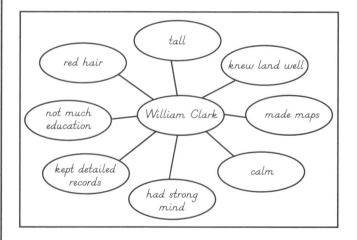

Sequence-of-Events Chain: Science

The chipmunk is in the middle of the food chain.

↓

The chipmunk eats nuts, grains, seeds, and insects.

↓

Chipmunks are food for many larger carnivores.

↓

When the larger carnivores die, decomposers return the nutrients to the soil.

↓

Plants use the nutrients in the soil to grow.

—From *Shining Star B* by Anna Uhl Chamot, Pamela Hartmann, and Jann Huizenga, Pearson Education, Inc., 2004. Reprinted with permission.

Use the format below to outline a SDAIE lesson for English learners. Include the strategies and activities you would include in each step. A blank template for planning a SDAIE lesson is provided on page 134 in the Resources section of this book.

PLANNING A SDAIE LESSON

Although there is no one formula for creating a SDAIE lesson, the planning guide below is useful in identifying the key elements and demonstrating the processes involved in SDAIE instruction. It can be adapted to any content area.

SDAIE LESSON PLANNING GUIDE

Lesson Topic/Title: _____

Learning Standard: _____
What content standard will this lesson support?

Learning Objectives: _____
What will students be able to do and to what degrees?

Key Concepts/Language/Vocabulary to Develop

Content Specific: The language and vocabulary that directly relate to the content to be learned. (This may be new to all students.)

Content Supportive: The language and vocabulary used in the lesson that support the content activity in terms of process, procedure, and so on. (This may be typically known to native English speakers but unfamiliar to English learners.)

Introduce
Prepare students to learn.

- *Experiences:* Identify and/or provide experiences that focus students, such as poems, music, literature, guest speakers, experiments, video, film, or field trips.

- *Prior knowledge:* Tap into/connect prior knowledge to current learning. Determine what students already know and identify misconceptions. Utilize brainstorming, K-W-L-H charts, or other graphic organizers.

Explore
Provide relevant instruction and practice.

- *Presentation:* Present information and develop concepts utilizing strategies that are appropriate to the content and English proficiency levels of the students. Utilize SDAIE strategies (scaffolds, graphic organizers, and cooperative/collaborative learning) and appropriate tools, materials, and resources. Modify materials and presentation to enhance comprehension and learning.

- *Practice:* Allow students opportunities to work independently, with partners, and in collaborative/ cooperative groups. Ensure that students are clear about the process and purpose of the activity.

Utilize varied grouping configurations and activities that appeal to a variety of learning styles. Monitor students, providing feedback, direction, and guidance as needed.

Extend
Provide opportunities and activities that extend, enrich, and integrate learning across the curriculum.

Focus on helping students make important conceptual and linguistic connections across the curriculum.

Assess
How will students demonstrate their learning? Continually monitor students by checking for clarification, observing concept and skill development, and modifying instruction to match student needs (ongoing assessment). In addition, determine the degree to which students have achieved the objectives of the lesson.

Students learn language and content best within meaningful contexts. Integrating the curriculum provides this context and serves to efficiently develop and connect seemingly diverse concepts and ideas while also developing the language that embodies them.

Integrated instruction also helps to manage the multilevel classroom. For example, the classroom is organized around a broad theme. Individual students or groups explore various topics (specific subsets of the theme) that are suited to their needs, interests, and abilities. Classroom resources, bulletin boards, field trips, art projects, and other activities emerge from the theme. The teacher can modify instructional activities to match the needs and interests of each group.

Integrated instruction for English learners can be viewed in two ways:

- Integrated English language development
- Integrated curriculum program

Integrated English Language Development

As discussed in Chapter 2, a balanced English language development (ELD) program includes activities characterized as literature, content, or communications based (and integrates into these activities listening, speaking, reading, writing, and higher-order thinking skills). The "core" lesson is enriched and extended by tying in related content area experiences. The primary purpose or goal of these content extensions is English language development. Content serves as the vehicle (much the way it is in content-based ELD).

Page 110 provides an example of an integrated ELD unit. Its focus is a literature piece titled "Seedfolks." Note the content extensions for the literary selection.

BRAINSTORM

Brainstorm extension activities for another piece of literature or topic. Use the Integrating Curriculum Web Template on page 132 to record the information.

Integrated Curriculum Program

An integrated program involves coordinating the entire instructional day around a specific theme. It has added requirements that provide structure and guidance, including:

- Identifying and incorporating the grade-level standards, goals, and objectives for each curricular area
- Organizing instruction and using appropriate strategies so that the individual academic and linguistic needs of all students are met
- Identifying and gathering resources and materials about the theme

In an integrated program, the theme serves as an organizing tool. The purpose of an integrated program is to develop grade-level core curriculum skills (much like SDAIE) in a way that helps students utilize the natural connections between the disciplines.

TIP Wise teachers point out that the theme must serve learning (not vice versa). Effective teachers dip in and out of the overarching class theme, bringing deeper meaning, insight, and skill to the big ideas and specific content areas. It is not always possible to integrate all needed teaching into the big theme. Side trips are occasionally made to explore other needed areas of learning.

INTEGRATING CURRICULUM WEB

Reading
- Shared reading of the text
- Individual or partner reading of the text
- Read additional short stories
- Read for details and literary elements
- Cloze exercise
- Conventions of print; cohesive devices
- Phonics word work and vocabulary work
- Read in groups of four, with each student reading designated segments within each paragraph

Music
- Listen to tape recording of selection
- Create song or rap to describe emotions of main characters
- Listen to traditional and modern music from Haiti

Math
- Calculate type and amount of materials needed to make a garden
- Determine costs of making a garden and how to allocate costs to those sharing the space
- Compare Fahrenheit and Celsius
- Problem solve how to create a garden cooperative

Listening
- To the story read aloud
- To the cassette tape
- To classroom plays or reader's theater
- Collaborative groups
- Pair work

Science
- Grow seeds
- Identify and label parts of growing seeds/plants
- Mix potting soil for specific purpose
- Plant garden
- Investigate seasonal crops
- Care for crops, including irrigation, pest management

SEEDFOLKS

Writing
- Realistic story
- New ending
- Description of character or point of view
- Rewrite as reader's theater or play
- Sequels/prequels

Social Studies
- Investigate country vs. city gardens and farms
- Design garden
- Explore local laws/regulations regarding community projects
- Research Haiti and the West Indies
- Interview a local successes

Thinking/Speaking
- Predict what will happen in the story
- Summarize the story
- Answer reference and display questions
- Retell the story in L1 and L2
- Features of language usage such as idioms, dialog
- Hot seat: Interview student who has taken on the role of a character
- Role-play

Art
- Masks or props for performances
- Collaborative mural of garden
- Design a locket or a book of garden photos or illustrations
- Paint a flower, landscape, or close-up of leaves
- Illustrate or create a goddess mosaic
- Illustrate new stories

Drama
- Reader's theater
- Perform a new ending or a new short story
- Write new plays

The more simplified or informal integration that occurs within an integrated ELD program serves as the basic structure or format for the more extensive integrated program. Integrating curriculum, in either case, is more than simply correlating topics. It is the careful integration of broad themes, or big ideas, that helps students make connections. Few problems in life are solved simply by applying knowledge from one distinct discipline. When students learn through thematic units:

- Learning is supported through contextualized instruction.
- Students gain insight and see the connectedness of concepts and ideas.
- Schema is developed and expanded as students utilize prior knowledge to construct new knowledge.
- Language is expanded through the natural redundancy that occurs when students connect familiar language and ideas to new information.

DIFFERENTIATING INSTRUCTION

The observation form on the next page outlines some of the most important behaviors, strategies, and supports necessary in providing meaningful instruction for English learners. Review the behaviors and reflect on the successful teaching experiences you have had or viewed.

TIP With a partner, use the list on page 112 to observe and record the teaching behaviors each of you use. Reflect on and discuss the observation notes. Identify and review the areas that are your strengths as well as the areas that need improvement.

LEARNING STYLES/MULTIPLE INTELLIGENCES

Learning styles are the preferred ways in which individuals receive and process information.[19] Students come to us with diverse styles of learning, which have traditionally been identified as visual, auditory, and kinesthetic. Howard Gardner's work[20] has extended this idea to the notion of intelligence, or rather "intelligences." Gardner believes that people have various areas of intelligence (*not* one overriding intelligence) that develop over time. These intelligences shape how a person learns and demonstrates knowledge.

Gardner affirms that although each identified intelligence is autonomous, intelligences work in harmony. Accomplishing tasks and solving problems typically require the orchestrated application of several intelligences. Gardner further explains that although these intelligences are demonstrated in a wide variety of cultures, they may manifest themselves differently in different cultures. How or whether an intelligence surfaces in an individual depends on at least two factors:[21]

Refer to page 113. Review the descriptions for each intelligence and determine your stronger intelligences. Then answer the following:

- *How have these intelligences helped you in school?*
- *How were these intelligences nurtured, encouraged, or rewarded?*
- *How could teachers have tapped into these intelligences to help you learn?*
- *How can you use this information to help all students learn?*

1. Biological predisposition to find or solve problems in a given domain
2. Whether the individual's culture elicits that predisposition or nurtures that domain

Focusing on and giving students time to nurture and develop their own intelligences results in students who are more apt to discover their own strengths, put more effort into improving their weak areas, and feel better about themselves.[22] If we can identify, appreciate, and provide learning opportunities that appeal to a variety of styles, or intelligences, we will go far to nurture intelligences and help students learn in ways that are the most meaningful to them.

DIFFERENTIATING INSTRUCTION
SUPPORTIVE CLASSROOM STRATEGIES

Classroom Environment
- Supportive environment
- Print rich with many visuals
- Reference charts
- Logical organization
- High expectations

Differentiated Instruction
- Utilize key visuals: sketches, diagrams, graphic organizers
- Use realia, authentic objects
- Rephrase/repeat key concepts
- Lesson delivery: speak clearly, use intonation, volume, and pauses to aid meaning
- Wait time—allow longer pause time for response
- Model/provide varied examples: language structures, patterns, procedures, finished products, and so on
- Check for comprehension
- Access prior knowledge
- Explicitly link prior learning and background knowledge to new learning
- Use questions and interactions to support and guide students to deeper understanding and learning
- Scaffold key concepts
- Provide multiple opportunities to demonstrate understanding
- Utilize formative assessment
- Be sure students are engaged
- Expect success for all students

Organization
- Grouping is purposeful
- Pacing is appropriate
- Meaningful independent work

Language Proficiency Level(s): _____

Notes: _____

_____

_____

_____

_____

_____

_____

_____

_____

_____

_____

_____

_____

_____

_____

_____

_____

_____

_____

_____

_____

_____

_____

_____

_____

_____

_____

_____

_____

Conference notes:

_____

_____

_____

_____

_____

HOW TO IDENTIFY AND NURTURE MULTIPLE INTELLIGENCES
MANY WAYS TO BE SMART!

LINGUISTIC 	*Sensitivity to words: their meaning, order, sounds, rhythm, and function. This intelligence is required of writers, orators, and those who appreciate them.* Focus on words—on saying them, hearing them, and using them. Provide opportunities for discussion, many and varied reading and writing tasks, and oral presentations. Encourage the use of storyboards, tape recorders, and computers. Visit libraries, bookstores, newspapers, publishers, and printers.
MUSICAL	*Sensitivity to pitch, rhythm, timbre, and the qualities of tone. This intelligence is required of composers, singers, conductors, and those who appreciate them.* Focus on rhythm, melody, and tone. Provide opportunities to listen and create music, play musical instruments, sing, compose, and dance. Attend concerts, musicals, music demonstrations, and visit recording studios.
LOGICAL-MATHEMATICAL 	*Ability to discern logical or numerical patterns, develop extended chains of reasoning, or handle increasingly abstract tiers of analysis. This intelligence is required of mathematicians, scientists, computer programmers, and individuals involved in finance-related businesses.* Focus on concept formation and finding relationships and patterns. Provide opportunities for experimentation, exploration, classification, categorization, and computer programming. Use games requiring strategy and logical analysis. Use science kits and lab materials. Visit museums of natural science, computer exhibits, banks, accounting firms.
SPATIAL	*Capacity to perceive forms and objects accurately, manipulate or mentally transform objects, or form mental images. Spatial intelligence is required of physicists, engineers, aarchitects, artists, mechanics, and chess players.* Focus on images, pictures, and color. Encourage visualization of problems. Provide opportunities for drawing, painting, and sculpting. Utilize multimedia, visuals, and realia. Visit art museums, planetariums, and architectual landmarks.
BODILY-KINESTHETIC	*Ability to handle objects and one's own body skillfully for functional or expressive purposes. This intelligence is demonstrated by skilled dancers, athletes, actors, surgeons, pianists, violinists, and other skilled craftspersons.* Focus on touching/manipulating objects, bodily movement. Provide opportunities for dramatization, pantomime, and other physical activities. Use playground and gymnasium equipment. Encourage hands-on arts and crafts activities. Visit campgrounds, art exhibits, and craft shows. Attend theatrical and dance presentations, and sporting events.
INDIVIDUAL (INTRAPERSONAL)	*Ability to understand oneself, including desires, goals, strengths, and weaknesses, and then act on this understanding. Individual intelligence is required to make appropriate life decisions.* Provide long-term meaningful projects. Encourage students to monitor and reflect on their own learning and explore their own interests and abilities. Give students choices in selecting and using materials. Encourage the use of portfolios.
SOCIAL (INTERPERSONAL) 	*Ability to distinguish moods, temperament, motivations, and intentions of others and to act on this knowledge. This intelligence is required of those who try to persuade others, such as political or religious leaders, managers, supervisors, counselors, teachers, and parents.* Encourage collaboration and interactions. Provide opportunities for group discussions, group problem solving, collaborative/cooperative projects and products, and peer teaching.

From *Nurturing Multiple Intelligences: A Guide to Multiple Intelligence Theory and Teaching,* by Brian Haggerty, © 1995. Reprinted by permission of Addison-Wesley Publishing Company.

Refer to and review the Preview page for this chapter (page 91). Was your prior knowledge accurate? (Did you have any misconceptions or inaccurate ideas?)

What did you LEARN about academic/content area development?

How can you apply this information? (Include one or two specific ideas.)

What else do you want to know?

NOTES

CHAPTER 5

Assessment and Evaluation

> *Tell the truth . . .*
>
> That is, indeed, the essence of effective standards and assessment. We tell the truth about what we expect of students. We tell the truth about the differences between their present performance and those standards. We tell the truth about the time and effort it will take to close that gap. And we tell the truth about the progress that students make toward the goals the community has established. Neither cryptic statistics nor evasive platitudes nor bromides about student self-esteem can meet this simple test of truth. Only a clear and direct statement about expectations and performance can meet such a test.
>
> Douglas B. Reeves, *Making Standards Work*[1]

Assessment has many purposes, including diagnosing student strengths and weaknesses, prescribing instruction and approaches, screening and selecting participants, identifying placement and progress, evaluating the effectiveness of a program, and assessing attitudes. In each purpose, seeking the truth about the student must remain central to the assessment.

This chapter will focus on assessment as a means for understanding the thinking of the student and also for determining the student's ability to effectively communicate that thinking in English through listening and speaking, reading, and writing. Assessment will be viewed in the following terms:

- Alignment with the authentic learning opportunities provided in the classroom
- Purpose in measuring what students can do
- Value as a tool for evaluating student needs and designing further instructional activities

What do you already KNOW about assessment and evaluation?

What do you WANT to know or learn?

ASSESSMENT PURPOSES

Assessment should be the servant of teaching and learning. Without information about their students' skills, understanding, and individual approaches . . . teachers have nothing to guide their work.

—J. Mokros, S. J. Russell, and K. Economopoulos,
Beyond Arithmetic[2]

Assessment in the classroom has many purposes but should maintain at its core the integration of assessment and instruction. The following diagram presents four purposes for assessment and the corresponding results.

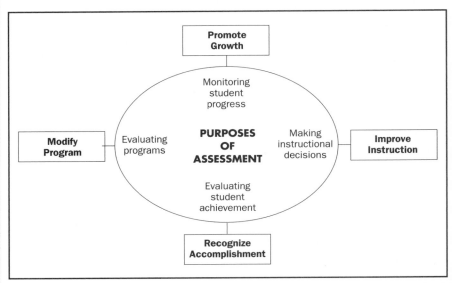

Reprinted with permission from *Assessment Standards for School Mathematics,* 1995, by the National Council of Teachers of Mathematics. All rights reserved.

Monitoring student progress: *Are students learning (understanding) what I am teaching? What is the evidence (demonstration) of their learning?* Assessment provides teachers and students with ongoing feedback concerning student progress toward meeting the established goals of the lesson and is used to inform instruction. Data are drawn primarily from demonstrations of students' learning: what they are thinking, doing, and saying—and how they are saying it.

Making instructional decisions: *Based on the evidence, what are my next instructional moves?* Assessment requires looking at the truth of students' learning and then making key decisions that will enhance instruction and provide students with greater opportunities to learn.

Evaluating student achievement: *To what degree did students learn? Did they achieve our goal?* Evaluation involves a teacher's judgment of how well students achieved the established standards or goals. It may involve test data, but it should also include a variety of information gathered during instructional time. Evaluation should assess what students know and understand and should not be used to compare students with one another.

Evaluating programs: *How well did my program work to achieve the goal?* In this case, a program is any organized system of instruction, practice, or curriculum. Assessment data are used to examine program effectiveness in terms of student learning and opportunities for learning and then to identify areas of needed improvement.[3]

If schools and schools systems are to continuously improve, they must measure growth in student achievement. After all, the goal of all activities in schools and school systems is teaching and learning, and the key question is: Are the students learning?

—U.S. Department of Education, *No Child Left Behind*[4]

THE ASSESSMENT CYCLE

Instruction should begin with, be supported by, and end with assessment. Assessment must be viewed as an integral part of day-to-day instruction, not just as a special culminating event. It is used to shape today's lesson and plan for tomorrow's. It is a process that involves: (1) setting goals, (2) gathering evidence to determine attainment of goals, (3) interpreting the evidence, and (4) using the new information to make decisions for teaching tomorrow. This process supports students in learning and teachers in teaching.[5] The following diagram illustrates the interrelationship between these four assessment elements that typically work in a cycle.

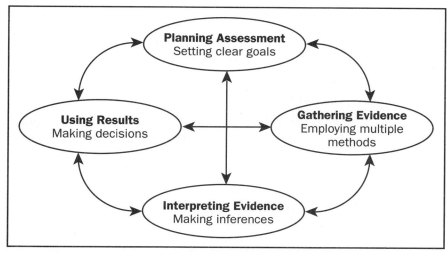

Reprinted with permission from *Assessment Standards for School Mathematics,* 1995, by the National Council of Teachers of Mathematics. All rights reserved.

BASIC PRINCIPLES OF ASSESSMENT

As noted previously, there are many purposes for assessment. There are, however, common basic principles that should be observed.

Child-Centered

Assessment should focus on students' strengths: what students can do, what they know, and how they have grown and progressed as English learners or "doers" of core curriculum.

Standards-Based

> *More than forty-five states have either implemented academic content standards or are in the process of developing them. The documents associated with these standards outline a set of expectations for the knowledge, performance, and achievement by students in the public schools of those states.*
>
> —Douglas B. Reeves, *Making Standards Work*[6]

Standards provide clear expectations for what students should *know and be able to do* and also *how well* they should be able to do them. With standards-based assessment, student work (products and performance) is measured by criteria that are directly linked to the established standards. Criteria include scales (or rubrics), performance, descriptions, and samples of student work (exemplars) that clearly differentiate the range of acceptable and unacceptable levels of performance. Together, these elements provide sources of evidence for documenting progress toward and attainment of the standards.[7] All students are measured against the same standard, not each other, and there is a presumption that all students can reach the standards.

Ongoing: Formative and Embedded

Assessment is a part of the daily activity of the classroom. It is embedded in the interactions teachers have with students and the careful observation of students as learners and users of English. Checking for clarification, monitoring instruction to match student needs, and asking comprehension questions are all examples of ongoing assessment. Ongoing assessment can be informal, as in the examples just mentioned, or formal. Formal ongoing assessment entails measuring progress at regular intervals and documenting student growth over time. A variety of tools can be used, such as portfolios, anecdotal notes, and established benchmarks and rubrics.

Summative

Summative evaluation tends to be more formal, assessing students after a specified period of time or after specific instructional activities. It measures the summation of learning, reflecting what has already been monitored and evaluated over time.

Formal and Informal

Assessment runs along a continuum from informal (observations, anecdotal notes, and clarification checks) to formal (testing instruments and performance tasks measured against a rubric). Formal and informal assessments both have value and should be incorporated in a student's overall program.

Involves the Student, Teacher, and Parents

Opportunities for student self-assessment and a developing sense of personal responsibility for learning should be part of assessment. Additionally, parents' involvement, including their perceptions of their children's strengths and talents and their expectations and concerns about the school, will prove invaluable in providing appropriate assessment and instruction. Parents should be invited to conferences and also to examine assessment information, such as portfolios, on a regular basis.

Varied

Providing a variety of assessment opportunities is important in order to get a complete picture of students' abilities and growth, as well as to avoid negative biases toward factors such as culture and learning styles. Further, varying assessment opportunities provides a clearer picture of the degree to which students have attained standards or proficiencies: Can students demonstrate knowledge and learning in a variety of contexts with flexibility or only within certain contexts?

PROVIDING A VARIETY OF ASSESSMENT OPPORTUNITIES

Assessment of core curriculum for English learners presents a significant challenge because measuring what students know and are able to do through English, their second language, is by its very nature also a measure of their proficiency in English. It is therefore particularly important that English learners be assessed using multiple measures and performance tasks that create a more complete picture of student content knowledge and understanding.

Assessment options range from standardized, skill-based instruments to more authentic assessment such as portfolios and performance-based assessments. To provide a complete evaluation of student knowledge, competence, or progress, a variety of assessment materials and opportunities should be utilized.

Portfolios

A portfolio should be more than a folder of student papers. It should tell a story that goes beyond the individual entries.
—John Van De Walle, *Elementary and Middle School Mathematics*[8]

Portfolio assessment is a focused, collaborative evaluation and analysis of the materials collected in a student's portfolio. The represented material is a meaningful collection of student work, gathered over time, that reflects learning with regard to instructional objectives[9] and represents the student's efforts, achievements, and personal, academic, and linguistic growth. Portfolio contents will vary considerably depending on the individual

TIP Encourage parents to identify areas of strength or interest that they have observed in the student. Use this information to design learning tasks that build on student strengths.

Identify the types of assessment opportunities you have provided. Describe the purposes and circumstances of the assessments.

TIP Determine the criteria by which items will be included in the student portfolio. To aid in interpreting the portfolio, include a description of the circumstances under which the entries were originally developed and the degree to which the work achieved the expected standards.

teacher and student goals. In addition to student work, portfolios may also contain informative materials from students, teachers, or parents, such as anecdotal records, self-assessments, checklists, scoring rubrics, audio or video recordings of student activities, parent/student questionnaires, student reflections, and peer conference reports.

Student portfolios are an excellent tool to use for parent conferencing. Parents are able to see concrete examples of their child's progress and contribute information from their unique perspectives.

Observation

TIP Watch for the conditions under which individuals seem to learn best. Keep this in mind as you plan instructional activities.

Student observations are done informally while monitoring classroom work and participation, and they can also be recorded on checklists or anecdotal records. "Kid-watching" is a powerful source of valuable information regarding what and how students are learning. Watch student behaviors in terms of English language—both quantity (fluency, amount of language) and quality (complexity of language, use of academic language)—and evidence of thinking and learning. Reflect on these observations to determine instructional needs.

Performance Tasks

Performance tasks require students to apply learned information or concepts to accomplish a task. The degree to which the task is accomplished (often measured against a benchmark or rubric) forms the basis of the assessment. Performance tasks are valuable in that they demonstrate what students can do in relation to specified objectives or standards.

Self-Assessment

TIP Using checklists for self-assessment is a simple way to develop this strategy.

TIP Have students complete a report card for themselves, including written comments. Students are likely to identify their own areas of struggle as well as areas of perceived weakness or strength.

As students reflect on and evaluate their own learning, they are developing a sense of personal responsibility and insight into their own strengths and talents. Accurate self-evaluation enhances self-esteem and promotes trust between teacher and student.[10] It is important that self-assessment reflect students' perceptions of themselves as learners. Questionnaires or open-ended writing prompts serve as effective self-assessment tools.[11]

Tests: Standardized/Skills Tests

Testing has been the traditional means of assessing student performance, and even with its limitations, testing will remain an important feature in educating students. Increasingly, students are facing high-stakes testing that has a direct impact on districts, schools, and the students themselves.

In December of 2001, Congress passed No Child Left Behind (NCLB) legislation requiring that states implement tests that "measure how well students meet the state's academic standards, which define what students should know and be able to do in different subject areas at different grade levels."[12] The aim of this required assessment is to improve student achievement and assist schools in identifying areas of need such as:

- Improving alignment between curriculum and state standards
- Modifying instructional methods
- Identifying areas of student need
- Clarifying areas that require professional development
- Providing information so that teachers can meet each student's needs

NCLB requires that all students be tested in reading or language arts, math, and soon, science. Although NCLB permits states to make "reasonable accommodations" for students with limited English proficiency, it does require that these subject-specific assessments be given in English to English learners who have been in a U.S. school for three consecutive years. In addition, states must ensure that English learners are tested on English proficiency in the areas of listening comprehension, reading, and writing skills in English.[13]

Teachers are cautioned against "teaching to the test" as discrete points and instead are encouraged to teach "the subject matter required by the standards, and teach it well . . . [so that] students will master the material on which they will be tested—and probably much more."[14] Another way to look at this is teaching the big ideas—the fundamental concepts and processes that underlie and connect standards. Students who have learned these conceptual ideas in a relational manner will tend to do well on tests regardless of test format.[15]

Test-Taking Strategies

With caution and some restraint, teachers can offer English learners some key test-taking strategies that can support them in taking tests. However, these strategies will not help students unless they have developed the knowledge and competence being assessed. Also, the time frame in which the specific test-taking strategies are taught should be shortly before the time of the actual test.[16] Provide students with experiences that include the test formats they are likely to encounter (for example, multiple choice) and specific language structures that carry significance (inference, opinion, "best answer," and so on). Teach specific testing tips:

- *Read each question carefully.* Understand what is being asked and what clues are provided in the question.
- *Anticipate the answer.* Predict or estimate the answer. Look at all choices and find the one that makes sense.
- *Eliminate choices.* Identify the choices that are clearly unreasonable.

Standardized instruments are also sources of valuable assessment information. They help in gauging students' progress both as a group and as individuals in relation to set critetia or standards or to their peers.

USING ASSESSMENT TOOLS

The following assessment tools are used independently and in varied combinations to supplement, reinforce, and validate assessment processes.

Anecdotal Records

Anecdotal records are descriptions of students' actions written as they occur or soon afterwards. The goal is to briefly transcribe what the student says or does and the context in which the behavior takes place. These accounts preserve a rich history of information about how a student learns and interacts in the school environment. In combination with portfolios and checklists, anecdotal records help teachers analyze a student's accomplishments and approach to learning over time.

TIP Have students use their primary language as a tool for understanding test questions. In particular, languages with Latin roots, such as Spanish, contain many everyday words and phrases that are cognates to more obscure English words often reserved for more academic contexts. For example:

- *infermo* (sick)—*infirm, infirmary*
- *masticar* (to chew)—*masticate*

TIP Use a clipboard and pages of adhesive labels. Write the observations on the labels, date them, and transfer them to the students' files.

Audio/Video Tapes

Taping what students actually do and say is an excellent means of documenting student behavior patterns and language development.

Logs or Journals

Student-produced learning logs or journals for reading, writing, or content learning serve to document students' language, literacy, and cognitive development and learning, as well as their ability to express this development and learning in informal writing. In addition, these tools serve to place reading and writing in a context that is functional and personally relevant. Students are often amazed to see their own growth and development over time.

Conferences

A conference is a time to meet and reflect on a student's work. It may involve the student, the teacher, and a parent. The student can take the lead in the conference, choosing pieces of work to discuss. Parents and teachers can offer their own observations and insights about particular works. Conferences provide a forum for students and teachers to set new learning goals together. Parents can also have input into this process.

Checklists

Checklists are tools for organizing and visually identifying the accomplishments of students in relation to specific learning objectives, skills, and behaviors. They give clear answers to clear questions. Checklists help teachers to manage information related to content, learning, and individual progress and then easily use the information to assess and evaluate student needs.

Rubrics

A scoring rubric is a rating scale that identifies the degree to which a student has met a specified standard. It can be very discrete, relating to a specific task (writing a letter), or broad in scope (development of oral language proficiency). Rubrics are valuable in identifying visible behaviors or traits that serve to measure growth and progress toward specified goals or standards. A general four-point rubric, such as the one on the facing page, identifies general categories of performance. It is also helpful to further develop these rubrics for the specific task by identifying specific performance indicators (examples) for each point of the rubric.

TIP Make sure students understand the purpose of a learning log or journal. (Its purpose may differ from daily writing or interactive journals.) Students should know that many people may be reading these journals.

TIP Use checklists to help ensure a balanced program of concept, language, and skill development.

SCORING WITH A FOUR-POINT RUBRIC

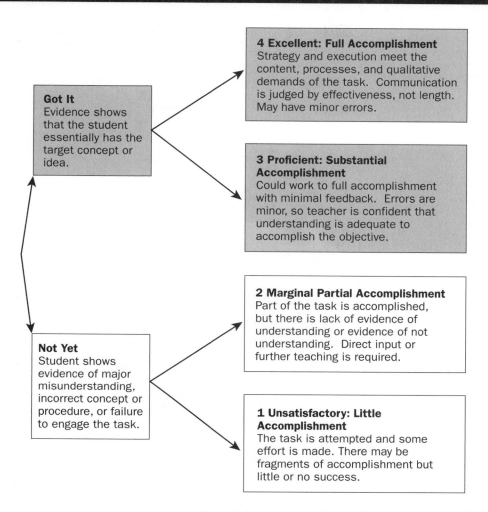

Got It
Evidence shows that the student essentially has the target concept or idea.

Not Yet
Student shows evidence of major misunderstanding, incorrect concept or procedure, or failure to engage the task.

4 Excellent: Full Accomplishment
Strategy and execution meet the content, processes, and qualitative demands of the task. Communication is judged by effectiveness, not length. May have minor errors.

3 Proficient: Substantial Accomplishment
Could work to full accomplishment with minimal feedback. Errors are minor, so teacher is confident that understanding is adequate to accomplish the objective.

2 Marginal Partial Accomplishment
Part of the task is accomplished, but there is lack of evidence of understanding or evidence of not understanding. Direct input or further teaching is required.

1 Unsatisfactory: Little Accomplishment
The task is attempted and some effort is made. There may be fragments of accomplishment but little or no success.

—From John A. Van de Walle, *Elementary and Middle School Mathematics: Teaching Developmentally,* 5th ed. Published by Allyn and Bacon, Boston, MA. Copyright © 2004 by Pearson Education. Reprinted by permission of publisher.

EVALUATION: MAKING JUDGMENTS

A fundamental goal of assessment is to *inform instruction*. If we clearly observe what students know and can do, we can then understand what must be taught next.[17] Evaluation is the process of analyzing assessment information to make judgments about student performance and suggest improvements or instructional modifications. Effective evaluation should answer these questions:

- *Where did the student begin?*
- *Where is the student going?*
- *Is the student finding success?*
- *If not, what changes should be made to meet student needs and ensure future success?*[18]

Using all assessment information—formal and informal, from portfolios to standardized and skills tests—provides balanced evaluation that conveys an accurate picture of student progress. With this clear picture, teachers are then equipped to modify, enrich, and customize instruction that accurately meets students' needs and moves them toward the full accomplishment of established academic goals.

Ultimately, assessment and evaluation are a search for the truth—the truth of how well students are learning and perhaps how well we are teaching them. This sometimes difficult truth can serve as the catalyst for improvement.

TIP Schedule regular opportunities (or use reporting periods) to reflect and complete this important evaluative task. Evaluation is a powerful tool in guiding appropriate instruction.

PORTFOLIO ASSESSMENT
Portfolio contents are one way to represent the student's linguistic achievements.

How do you provide for student evaluation?

Refer to and review the Preview page for this chapter (page 117). Was your prior knowledge accurate? (Did you have any misconceptions or inaccurate ideas?)

What did you LEARN about assessment and evaluation?

How can you apply this information? (Include one or two specific ideas.)

What else do you want to know?

RESOURCE PAGES

STANDARDS-BASED ELD PLANNING GUIDE

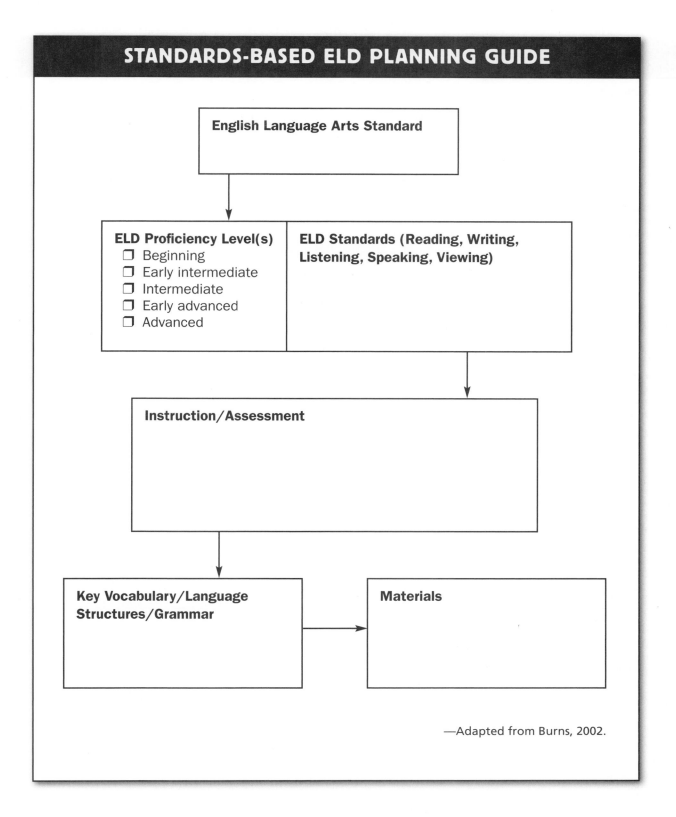

English Language Arts Standard

ELD Proficiency Level(s)
- ☐ Beginning
- ☐ Early intermediate
- ☐ Intermediate
- ☐ Early advanced
- ☐ Advanced

ELD Standards (Reading, Writing, Listening, Speaking, Viewing)

Instruction/Assessment

Key Vocabulary/Language Structures/Grammar

Materials

—Adapted from Burns, 2002.

ANALYZING TEXT

Title, Author, (Level)	
Genre	
Structure • *Narrative* • *Expository*	
Content/Themes/Ideas	
Strategies for Making Meaning	
Levels of Comprehension • *Literal* • *Inferential* • *Applied*	
Prior Knowledge • *Linguistic* • *Cultural* • *Experiential*	
Literary Features/Devices • *Perspective/Point of view* • *Dialog* • *Chronology*	
Language Features/Devices • *Vocabulary* • *Idioms, figurative language* • *Structures and patterns* • *Complexity*	
Language Cohesion • *Reference* • *Substitution* • *Ellipses* • *Conjunctions* • *Lexical cohesion*	
Engagement/Opportunities to • *Talk* • *Reflect*	
Book/Print Features • *Length/Organization* • *Font* • *Layout* • *Visuals*	
Additional Supports/Challenges	

—Adapted from Messiano, 2002, and Fountas and Pinnell, 2002.

WORD FORMS

Noun	Adjective	Verb	Adverb

INTEGRATING CURRICULUM WEB TEMPLATE

Reading

Music

Math

Listening

Science

Writing

Social Studies

Thinking/Speaking

Art

Drama

LITERARY INNOVATIONS

New Content

_____
_____
_____
_____
_____
_____
_____

New Titles

_____
_____
_____
_____
_____
_____

ORIGINAL STORY

New Story Lines

_____
_____
_____
_____
_____
_____
_____

New Characters

_____
_____
_____
_____
_____
_____
_____

SDAIE LESSON PLANNING GUIDE

Lesson Topic/Title: _____

Learning Standard: _____
What content standard will this lesson support?

Learning Objectives: _____
What will students be able to do and to what degrees?

Key Concepts/Language/Vocabulary to Develop

    Content Specific: _____

    _____

    Content Supportive: _____

    _____

Introduce	Materials
Explore	
Extend	
Assess	

CHAPTER NOTES

Chapter 1

1. Olsen and Chen. 1988, p. 3.
2. Cummins, 2000, 1984; Skutnabb-Kangas, 2000.
3. Cummins, 2000, 1989; Skutnabb-Kangas, 1984; Ramirez, 1992.
4. Walqui, 2000; Cummins, 2000, 1981.
5. Meyers, 1993.
6. Walqui, 1995.
7. Hymes, 1974.
8. Rubin, 1975.
9. Ginott, 1976, p. 13.
10. Traill, 1989.
11. Thoele, 1991.
12. Cummins, 2000, 1989.

Chapter 2

1. California Department of Education, 1992.
2. Walqui, 1993b.
3. Canale, 1983; Cummins, 2000; Citizenship and Immigration Canada, 1996.
4. Gibbons, 2002, p.2.
5. Gibbons, 2002.
6. Gibbons, 2002.
7. Cummins, 2000, 1984.
8. Cummins, 2000, 1984.
9. Cummins, 1981.
10. Cummins, 2000, 1981.
11. Wong-Fillmore, 1991.
12. Krashen and Terrell, 1983.
13. Walqui, 2000.
14. August and Hakuta, 1998; Thomas and Collier, 1997; Hakuta, Butler, and Witt, 2000.
15. California Department of Education, 1999.
16. California Department of Education, 2000.
17. Cummins, 2000; Saunders et al., 1999.
18. Cummins, 2000; Walqui, 2000.
19. Long and Crookes, 1992.
20. Krashen, 1981; Krashen and Terrell, 1983.
21. Cummins, 2000, 1993; Vincent, 1996; Long, 1982; Kagen, 1986; Enright and McCloskey, 1988.
22. Mercer, 2000, 1995; Gibbons, 2002.
23. Cummins, 1993.
24. Gibbons, 2002.
25. Collier, 1987; Krashen et al., 1979.
26. Cummins, 1981; McLaughlin 1992.
27. Walqui, 2000.
28. Richard-Amato, 1988.
29. Krashen, 1981.
30. Crawford, 1999, p. 102.
31. Long, 1982; Gibbons, 2002.
32. Diaz-Rico and Weed, 1995.
33. Diaz-Rico and Weed, 1995, p. 79.
34. Yorio, 1980.
35. Diaz-Rico and Weed, 1995, p. 80
36. Scarcella, 2000.
37. Fletcher and Portalupi, 1998, p. 51.
38. California Department of Education, 1992, p. 17.
39. Holdaway, 1986.
40. Routman, 1991.
41. Long and Crookes, 1992.
42. Asher, 1982.
43. Harris and Carr, 1996; California Department of Education, 2000.
44. California Department of Education, 1999.
45. Burns, 2002.
46. Lapp, Flood, and Tinajero, 1994.
47. Lapp, Flood, and Tinajero, 1994.
48. Kobrin, 2000.
49. Harvey, 2000.

Chapter 3

1. D. Easton, in California Department of Education, 2000, p. v.
2. In Gibbons, 1993, p. 70.
3. Gibbons, 1993, p. 71.
4. Goodman, 1968.
5. Routman, 1991.
6. Routman, 1991.
7. California Department of Education, 2000, p. 10.
8. Harvey and Goudvis, 2000, p. 5.
9. California Department of Education, 2000; Harvey and Goudvis, 2000; Pearson et al., 1992; Keene and Zimmerman, 1997.
10. Fountas and Pinnell, 1996; Paul, 1996; California Department of Education, 2000; Chamot and O'Malley, 1994; Harvey and Goudvis, 2000.
11. Cambourne, 1988.
12. Cambourne, 1988.
13. Honig, 1995.
14. California Department of Education, 1992, p. 4.

15. Adams and Bruck, 1995.
16. Holdaway, 1979; Routman, 1991; Fountas and Pinnell, 2001.
17. Parkes, 2000.
18. Cunningham, 1995, 2000.
19. Wilhelm, 2001.
20. Fountas and Pinnell, 2001.
21. Mooney, 1990.
22. Fountas and Pinnell, 2001, 1999, 1996; Pinnell and Fountas, 2002.
23. Fountas and Pinnell, 1999, p. 12.
24. *Education Week,* February 17, 1999, p. 16.
25. Allington, 2001.
26. Mooney, 1990, p. 11.
27. Fountas and Pinnell, 2001.
28. Calkins, 2001, p. 102.
29. Calkins, 2001.
30. Atwell, 1987; Calkins, 2001, 1991; Schell, 1995.
31. Gibbons, 2002.
32. McMillan, 1995.
33. Tinajero and Calderon, 1988; Van Allen, 1973; Walter, 1995.
34. Sweet, 1993.
35. Fisher, 1995.
36. Willis, 1995.
37. California Department of Education, 2000.
38. Honig, 1995.
39. Snow, Burns, and Griffin, 1998; Cummins, 1981.
40. Kinsella, 2001b.
41. Diaz-Rico and Weed, 1995; Gibbons, 1993.
42. Gibbons, 1993, p. 84.
43. Gibbons, 1993, p. 87.
44. Treadway, 1995, 1989.
45. Wilhelm, 2001.
46. Swartz, Klein, and Shook, 2001, p. vi.
47. Swartz, Klein, and Shook, 2001; McCarrier, Pinnell, and Fountas, 2000.
48. Heald-Taylor, 1997.
49. Nasdijj, in Fletcher and Portalupi, 2001, p. 130.
50. Fletcher and Portalupi, 2001, p. 130
51. Fletcher and Portalupi, 2001; Atwell, 1987; Calkins, 1991; Schell, 1995.
52. Fletcher and Portalupi, 2001, p. 10–11.
53. Fletcher, 1996, p. 3.
54. Ray, 2002.
55. Calkins, 2001, p. 493.
56. Johnson and Louis, 1987.

Chapter 4

1. Genesee, 1994, p. 3.
2. Walqui, 2000, p. 42.
3. Walqui, 1995.
4. Vygotsky, 1978.
5. Walqui, 2000, p. 42.
6. Walqui, 1995.
7. Walqui, 2001, p. 9.
8. Sobul, 1994.
9. Law and Eckes, 1990.
10. Walqui, 1993a, p. 6.
11. Faltis, 1993; Walqui, 2001, 1993a.
12. Walqui, 1993a.
13. Kinsella, 2001a.
14. Richard-Amato and Snow, 1992, in Diaz-Rico and Weed, 1995, p. 122.
15. Chamot and O'Malley, 1994, 1986; Chamot et al., 1999.
16. Meyers, 1993, p. 72.
17. Kagen, 1986; Johnson and Johnson, 1985.
18. Meyers, 1993, pp. 73–74.
19. Meyers, 1993.
20. Gardner, 1999, 1985.
21. Haggerty, 1996.
22. Nelson, 1995.

Chapter 5

1. Reeves, 1998, p. 77.
2. Mokros, Russell, and Economopoulos, 1995, p. 84.
3. Van De Walle, 2004.
4. U.S. Department of Education, 2003, p. 27.
5. Van De Walle, 2004.
6. Reeves, 1998, p. 33.
7. Harris and Carr, 1996.
8. Van De Walle, 2004, p. 74.
9. O'Malley and Valdez Pierce, 1996.
10. Eisele, 1991.
11. Van De Walle, 2004.
12. U.S. Department of Education, 2003, p. 27.
13. U.S. Department of Education, 2003.
14. U.S. Department of Education, 2003, p. 27.
15. Van de Walle, 2004.
16. Van de Walle, 2004.
17. Fisette, 1993.
18. Eisele, 1991.

REFERENCES

Adams, M., and Bruck, M. (1995). Learning to Read: Resolving the Great Debate. *American Federation of Teachers,* Summer, 1995.

Allington, Richard (2001). *What Really Matters for Struggling Readers: Designing Research-Based Programs.* Boston: Addison-Wesley.

Asher, J. (1982). *Learning Another Language Through Actions: The Complete Teachers' Guidebook.* Los Gatos, CA: Sky Oaks.

Atwell, N. (1987). *In the Middle: Writing, Reading, and Learning with Adolescents.* Portsmouth, NH: Heinemann.

August, Diane, and Hakuta, Kenji (1998). *Educating Language Minority Children.* Washington DC: National Academy Press.

Banks, James A. (1988). *Multiethnic Education: Theory and Practice,* Second Edition. Boston: Allyn and Bacon.

Bennett, Christine (1990). *Comprehensive Multicultural Education.* Boston: Allyn and Bacon.

Burns, Gaye (2002). Standards-Based Lesson Planning for ELD. In *ELD/SDAIE Training for Elementary Teachers.* San Diego, CA: San Diego City Schools.

California Department of Education (1992). *It's Elementary: Elementary Grades Task Force Report.* Sacramento, CA: California State Department of Education.

California Department of Education (1999). *English Language Development Standards.* Sacramento, CA: Standards, Curriculum, and Assessment Division, California Department of Education.

California Department of Education (2000). *Strategic Teaching and Learning: Standard-Based Instruction to Promote Content Literacy in Grades Four Through Twelve.* Sacramento, CA: California Department of Education.

California Department of Education, Bilingual Education Office (1986). *Beyond Language: Social and Cultural Factors in Schooling Language Minority Students.* Los Angeles: California State University.

Calkins, Lucy McCormick (1991). *Living Between the Lines.* Portsmouth, NH: Heinemann.

Calkins, Lucy McCormick (2001). *The Art of Teaching Reading.* MA: Addison-Wesley.

Cambourne, B. (1988). *The Whole Story: Natural Learning and the Acquisition of Literacy in the Classroom.* Richmond Hill, Ontario: Scholastic-TAB.

Canale, M. (1983). From Communicative Competence to Communicative Language Pedagogy. In J. Richards and R. Schmidt (eds.), *Language and Communication.* New York: Longman.

Chamot, A. U., and O'Malley, J. M. (1986). *A Cognitive Academic Language Learning Approach: An ESL Content-based Curriculum.* Washington, DC: National Clearinghouse for Bilingual Education.

Chamot, A. U., and O'Malley, J. M. (1987). The Cognitive Academic Language Learning Approach: A Bridge to the Mainstream. *TESOL Quarterly,* 21(2): 238.

Chamot, A. U., and O'Malley, J. M. (1994). *The CALLA Handbook: Implementing the Cognitive Academic Language Learning Approach.* Reading, MA: Addison-Wesley.

Chamot, A. U., Barhardt, S., El-Dinary, P. B., and Robbins, J. (1999). *The Learning Strategies Handbook.* White Plains, NY: Longman.

Chesterfield, R., and Chesterfield, K. (1985). Natural Order in Children's Use of Second Language Learning Strategies. *Applied Linguistics,* 6:45–59.

Citizenship and Immigration Canada (1996). *Canadian Benchmarks. Working Document.* Ottawa: Ministry of Supply and Services Canada.

Collier, V. (1987). Age and Rate of Acquisition of Second Language for Academic Purposes. *TESOL Quarterly,* 21(4): 617–641.

Crawford, James. (1999). *Bilingual Education: History, Politics, Theory, and Practice,* Fourth Edition. Los Angeles, CA: Bilingual Educational Services.

Cummins, J. (1981). The Role of Primary Language Development in Promoting Educational Success for Language Minority Students. In *Schooling and Language Minority Students: A Theoretical Framework.* Sacramento, CA: California State Department of Education.

Cummins, J. (1984). *Bilingualism and Special Education: Issues in Assessment and Pedagogy.* San Diego, CA: College-Hill.

Cummins, J. (1989). *Empowering Minority Students.* Sacramento, CA: California Association for Bilingual Education.

Cummins, J. (1993). *The Acquisition of English as a Second Language.* Presentation article/handout for California Elementary Education Association, San Diego.

Cummins, J. (2000). *Language, Power, and Pedagogy: Bilingual Education in the Crossfire.* Clevedon, England: Multilingual Matters LTD.

Cunningham, Patricia (1995, 2000). *Phonics They Use.* New York: HarperCollins.

Denton, D. (1988). *Whole Language: The Beginning . . . The Middle . . . Never Ending!* Handout presented at Longfellow Elementary School, San Diego, CA.

Diaz-Rico, L., and Weed, K. (1995). *The Crosscultural, Language, and Academic Development Handbook.* Needham Heights, MA: Allyn and Bacon.

Education Week. February 17, 1999, p. 16. In Allington, 2001, p. 27.

Eisele, Beverly (1991). *Managing the Whole Language Classroom.* Cypress, CA: Creative Teaching Press.

Enright, D., and McCloskey, M. (1988). *Integrating English: Developing English Language and Literacy in the Multilingual Classroom.* Reading, MA: Addison-Wesley.

Faltis, C. (1993). *JOINFOSTERING: Adapting Teaching Strategies for the Multilingual Classroom.* New York: Macmillan.

Fisette, D. (1993). Practical Authentic Assessment: Good Kid Watchers Know What to Teach Next! *The California Reader,* 26(4): 4–9.

Fisher, B. (1995). We *Do* Teach Phonics. *Teaching K–8,* September.

Fletcher, Ralph. (1996). *A Writer's Notebook: Unlocking the Writer Within You.* New York: Avon Books.

Fletcher, Ralph, and Portalupi, Joann (1998). *Craft Lessons: Teaching Writing K–8.* Portland, ME: Stenhouse Publishers.

Fletcher, Ralph, and Portalupi, Joann (eds.) (2001). *Writing Workshop: The Essential Guide.* New York: Heinemann.

Fountas, Irene C., and Pinnell, Gay Su (1996). *Guided Reading.* Portsmouth, NH: Heinemann.

Fountas, Irene C., and Pinnell, Gay Su (1999). *Matching Books to Readers.* Portsmouth, NH: Heinemann.

Fountas, Irene C., and Pinnell, Gay Su (2001). *Guiding Readers and Writers Grades 3–6.* Portsmouth, NH: Heinemann.

Gardner, H. (1985). *Frames of Mind: The Theory of Multiple Intelligences.* New York: HarperCollins.

Gardner, H. (1999). *Intelligence Reframed: Multiple Intelligences for the 21st Century.* New York: Basic Books.

Genesee, Fred (1994). *Integrating Language and Content: Lessons from Immersion.* National Center for Research on Cultural Diversity and Second Language Learning. Educational Practice Report: 11, p. 3.

Gibbons, Pauline (1993). *Learning to Learn in a Second Language.* Portsmouth, NH: Heinemann.

Gibbons, Pauline (2002). *Scaffolding Language, Scaffolding Learning: Teaching Second Language Learners in the Mainstream Classroom.* Portsmouth, NH: Heinemann.

Ginott, Haim (1976). *Between Teacher and Child.* New York: Morrow/Avon.

Goodman, K. (1968). *The Psycholinguistic Nature of the Reading Process.* Detroit, MI: Wayne State University Press.

Griffith, Ro (ed.) (1997). *Reading for Life.* Wellington, NZ: Learning Media Limited.

Hakuta, Kenji, Butler, Yuko Goto, and Witt, Daria (2000). *How Long Does It Take English Learners to Attain Proficiency?* The University of California Linguistic Minority Research Institute Policy Report 2001-1, Stanford University, CA.

Haggerty, Brian (1995). *Nurturing Intelligences: A Guide to Multiple Intelligence Theory and Teaching.* Reading, MA: Addison-Wesley.

Haggerty, Brian (1996). *Nurturing Intelligences: Core Literature Series: Teaching Guide to Russell Freedman's Lincoln: A Photobiography.* Reading, MA: Addison-Wesley.

Harris, Douglas E., and Carr, Judy F. (1996). *How to Use Standards in the Classroom.* Alexandria, VA: Association for Supervision and Curriculum Development.

Harvey, Stephanie (ed.) (2000). *Nonfiction Matters: Reading, Writing, and Research in Grades 3–8.* York, ME: Stenhouse.

Harvey, Stephanie, and Goudvis, Anne (2000). *Strategies That Work.* York, ME: Stenhouse Publishers.

Heald-Taylor, Gail (1997). *Whole Language Strategies for ESL Students.* Toronto, Canada: University of Toronto Press.

Holdaway, D. (1979). *The Foundations of Literacy.* Portsmouth, NH: Heinemann.

Holdaway, D. (1986). In Michael Sampson (ed.), *The Pursuit of Literacy: Early Reading and Writing.* Dubuque, IA: Kendall/Hunt Publishing.

Honig, B. (1995). *How Should We Teach Our Children to Read? A Balanced Approach.* (Pre-publication draft).

Hymes, D. (1974). *Directions in Sociolinguistics.* Philadelphia: University of Pennsylvania Press.

Johnson, D. W., and Johnson, R. T. (1985). *Structuring Cooperative Learning: Lesson Plans for Teachers.* Edina, MN: Interaction.

Johnson, D. W., Johnson, R. T., and Holubec, E. J. (1986). *Circles of Learning: Cooperation in the Classroom,* Revised. Edina, MN: Interaction.

Johnson, T., and Louis, D. (1987). *Literacy Through Literature.* Portsmouth, NH: Heinemann.

Kagen, S. (1986). Cooperative Learning and Sociocultural Factors in Schooling. In *Beyond Language: Social and Cultural Factors in Schooling Language Minority Students.* Sacramento, CA: California State Department of Education.

Keene, Ellin L., and Susan Zimmerman (1997). *Mosaic of Thought: Teaching Comprehension in a Reader's Workshop.* Portsmouth, NH: Heinemann.

Kinsella, Kate (2001a). *Expository Writing Scaffolds for English Learners in Content Area Classrooms.* Presentation article/handout for Standards-Based Evaluation and Accountability Institute for English Learners. California Department of Education, Santa Barbara, CA.

Kinsella, Kate (2001b). *Academic Vocabulary Development to Support Reading and Learning from Texts.* Presentation article/handout for Standards-Based Evaluation and Accountability Institute for English Learners. California Department of Education, Santa Barbara, CA.

Kobrin, Beverly (2000). In S. Harvey (ed.), *Nonfiction Matters: Reading, Writing, and Research in Grades 3–8.* York, ME: Stenhouse.

Krashen, Steven (1981). Bilingual Education and Second Language Acquisition Theory. In *Schooling and Language Minority Students: A Theoretical Framework.* Sacramento, CA: California State Department of Education.

Krashen, Steven (1993). *The Power of Reading.* Englewood, CO: Libraries Unlimited.

Krashen, S., Long, M., and Scarcella, R. (1979). Age, Rate, and Eventual Attainment in Second Language Acquisition. *TESOL Quarterly,* 13(4): 573–582.

Krashen, S., and Terrell, T. (1983) *The Natural Approach.* Hayward, CA: Alemany Press.

Lapp, D., Flood, J., and Tinajero, J. (1994). Are We Communicating? Effective Instruction for Students Who Are Acquiring English as a Second Language. *The Reading Teacher,* 48(3): 260–264.

Law, B., and Eckes, M. (1990). *The More Than Just Surviving Handbook: ESL for Every Classroom Teacher.* Winnipeg, Canada: Penguin.

Long, M. (1982). Input, Interaction, and Second Language Acquisition. *TESOL Quarterly,* 19(2): 207–225.

Long, M., and Crookes G. (1992). Three Approaches to Task-Based Syllabus Design. *TESOL Quarterly,* 26(1): 27–56.

McCarrier, Andrea, Pinnell, Gay Su, and Fountas, Irene (2000). *Interactive Writing: How Language and Literacy Come Together, K–2.* Portsmouth, NH: Heinemann.

McLaughlin, Barry (1992). *Myths and Misconceptions About Second Language Learning: What Every Teachers Needs to Unlearn.* Educational Research Report 5. The National Center for Research on Cultural Diversity and Second Language Learning, University of California, Santa Cruz.

McMillan, S. (1995). In *English Learner Achievement Project (ELAP) Training Handbook.* San Diego, CA: San Diego City Schools.

Mercer, N. (1995). *The Guided Construction of Knowledge: Talk Amongst Teachers and Learners.* Clevedon, UK: Multilingual Matters.

Mercer, N. (2000). *Words and Minds: How We Use Language to Think Together.* London: Routledge.

Messiano, Rita (2002). *Analyzing Text.* Presentation handout, San Diego City Schools Literacy Institute. San Diego, CA.

Meyers, Mary (1993). *Teaching to Diversity: Teaching and Learning in the Multi-Ethnic Classroom.* Toronto: Irwin. (U.S. Edition, Reading, MA: Addison-Wesley.)

Mokros, J., Russell, S. J., and Economopoulos, K. (1995). *Beyond Arithmetic: Changing Mathematics in the Elementary Classroom.* Palo Alto, CA: Dale Seymour.

Mooney, M. (1990). *Reading To, With, and By Children.* Katonah, NY: Richard Owen.

Mooney, M. (1995). Guided Reading Beyond the Primary Grades. *Teaching K–8,* September; *Instructor,* July/August.

Nasdijj (2001). In Ralph Fletcher and Joann Portalupi (eds.), *Writing Workshop: The Essential Guide.* New York: Heinemann.

National Council of Teachers of Mathematics (1995). *Assessment Standards for School Mathematics.* Reston, VA: Author.

National Council of Teachers of Mathematics (2000). *Principles and Standards for School Mathematics.* Reston, VA: Author.

Nelson, K. (1995). Nurturing Kids: Seven Ways of Being Smart. *Instructor,* July/August.

Olsen, L., and Chen, T. (1988). *The World Enrolls.* San Francisco: California Tomorrow.

O'Malley, J. M., and Valdez Pierce, L. (1996). *Authentic Assessment for English Language Learners: Practical Strategies for Teachers.* Reading, MA: Addison-Wesley.

Paul, Terrance, D. (1996). *Patterns of Reading Practice.* Madison, WI: Institute for Academic Excellence.

Parkes, Brenda (2000). *Read It Again! Revisiting Shared Reading.* Portland, ME: Stenhouse.

Pearson, P. David, Roehler, L. R., Doyle, J. A., and Duffy, G. G. (1992). Developing Expertise in Reading Comprehension. In J. Samuels and A. Farstrup (eds.), *What Research Has to Say About Reading Instruction.* Newark, DE: International Reading Association.

Pinnell, Gay Su, and Fountas, Irene C. (2002). *Leveled Books for Readers Grades 3–6.* Portsmouth, NH: Heinemann.

Ramirez, J. (1992). Executive Summary, Final Report: Longitudinal Study of Structured Immersion Strategy, Early-Exit and Late-Exit Transitional Bilingual Education Programs for Language-Minority Children. *Bilingual Research Journal,* 16(1, 2): 1–62.

Ray, Katie Wood (2002). *What You Know by Heart: How to Develop Curriculum for Your Writing Workshop.* Portsmouth, NH: Heinemann.

Reeves, Douglas B. (1998). *Making Standards Work: How to Implement Standards-Based Assessments in the Classroom, School, and District.* Denver, CO: Center for Performance Assessment.

Richard-Amato, P. (1988). *Making It Happen.* White Plains, NY: Longman.

Richard-Amato, P., and Snow, Marguerite Ann (eds.) (1992). *The Multicultural Classroom.* White Plains, NY: Longman.

Routman, R. (1991) *Invitations.* Portsmouth. NH: Heinemann.

Rubin, J. (1975). What the Good Language Learner Can Teach Us. *TESOL Quarterly,* 9:41–51.

Rubin, J., and Thompson, I. (1982). *How to Be a More Successful Language Learner.* Boston: Heinle and Heinle.

Saunders, W., O'Brien, G., Lenon, D., and McLean, J. (1999). *Successful Transition into Mainstream English: Effective Strategies for Studying Literature.* Santa Cruz, CA: Center for Research on Education, Diversity, and Excellence.

Scarcella, Robin (2000). *Ten Instructional Points.* Presentation article/handout for *Standards-Based Evaluation and Accountability Institute for English Learners.* California Department of Education, Santa Barbara.

Schell, E. (1995). The Workshop Approach to Reading, Writing, and History. In *English Learner Achievement Project (ELAP) Training Handbook.* San Diego: San Diego City Schools.

Skutnabb-Kangas, T. (1984). *Bilingualism or Not: The Education of Minorities.* Clevedon, England: Multilingual Matters.

Skutnabb-Kangas, T. (2000). *Linguistic Genocide in Education—or Worldwide Diversity and Human Rights.* Mawah, NJ: Erlbaum.

Smith, F. (1971). *Understanding Reading.* Toronto: Holt, Rinehart & Winston.

Snow, Catherine, Burns, M. Susan, and Griffin, Peg (1998). *Preventing Reading Difficulties in Young Children.* Washington DC: National Academy Press.

Sobul, D. (1994). *Strategies to Meet the Goals of SDAIE.* Presentation at California Association of Bilingual Education, San Jose.

Swartz, S., Klein, A., and Shook, R. (2001). *Interactive Writing and Interactive Editing: Making Connections Between Writing and Reading.* Carlsbad, CA: Dominie Press.

Sweet, A. (1993). *State of the Art: Transforming Ideas for Teaching and Learning to Read.* Washington, DC: U.S. Department of Education, U.S. Government Printing Office.

Terrell, T. (1981). The Natural Approach in Bilingual Education. In *Schooling and Language Minority Students: A Theoretical Framework.* Sacramento, CA: California State Department of Education.

Thoele, S. Patton (1991). Making a Difference. In *The Woman's Book of Courage.* Berkeley, CA: Conari Press.

Thomas, W. P,. and Collier, V. (1997). *School Effectiveness for Language Minority Students.* Washington, DC: National Clearinghouse for Bilingual Education.

Tiedt, P., and Tiedt, I. (1979). *Multicultural Teaching: A Handbook of Activities, Information, and Resources.* Boston: Allyn and Bacon.

Tinajero, J., and Calderon, M. (1988). Language Experience Approach Plus. *Journal of Educational Issues of Language Minority Students,* 2: 31–45.

Traill, Leanna (1989). Classroom Environment and Organization. Presentation handout, San Diego County Department of Education, San Diego, CA.

Treadway, J. (1989). The Directed Reading-Thinking Activity. *Learning Magazine,* April: 56–57.

Treadway, J. (1995). *Directed Reading-Thinking Activities.* Presentation at Mann Middle School, San Diego, CA.

U.S. Department of Education (2003). *No Child Left Behind: A Toolkit for Teachers.* Jessup, MD: Education Publishing Center.

Van Allen, R. (1973). The Language Experience Approach. In R. Karlen (ed.), *Perspectives on Elementary Reading: Principles and Strategies of Teaching.* New York: Harcourt Brace Jovanovich.

Van de Walle, John A. (2004). *Elementary and Middle School Mathematics: Teaching Developmentally,* Fifth Edition. Boston, MA: Pearson Education.

Vincent, C. (1996). *Singing to a Star: The School Meaning of Second Generation Salvadorean Students.* Doctoral dissertation, George Mason University, Farifax, VA.

Vygotsksy, L. S. (1978). *Mind in Society.* Cambridge, MA: Harvard University Press.

Walqui, Aida (1993a) Sheltered Instruction: Doing It Right. In *Bilingual Teacher Training Program: Sheltered Instruction Institute.* San Diego, CA: San Diego County Office of Education.

Walqui, Aida (1993b). Literature Review: Sheltered Instruction. In *Bilingual Teacher Training Program: Sheltered Instruction Institute.* San Diego, CA: San Diego County Office of Education.

Walqui, Aida (1995). Presentation. *Bilingual Teacher Training Program: Sheltered Instruction Institute.* San Diego, CA: San Diego County Office of Education.

Walqui, Aida (2000). *Access and Engagement: Program Design and Instructional Approaches for Immigrant Students in Secondary School.* McHenry, IL: Center for Applied Linguistics, and Delta Systems.

Walqui, Aida (2001). *Academic Language: The Development of a Theoretical Construct and Its Applications.* Keynote presentation handout. Santa Barbara, CA: California Department of Education Institute on Evaluation and Accountability for English Language Learners.

Walter, T. (1995). In *English Learner Achievement Project (ELAP) Training Handbook.* San Diego, CA: San Diego City Schools.

Willis, S. (1995). Whole Language: Finding the Surest Way to Literacy. *Curriculum Update* (Fall). Alexandria, VA: Association for Supervision and Curriculum Development.

Wilhelm, J. (2001). *Improving Comprehension with Think-Aloud Strategies.* New York: Scholastic.

Wong-Fillmore, L. (1991). Second Language Learning in Children: A Model of Language Learning in a Social Context. In E. Bialystok (ed.), *Language Processing in Bilingual Children.* Cambridge, England: Cambridge University Press, pp. 49–69.

Yorio, C. (1980). The Teacher's Attitude Toward the Student's Output in the Second Language Classroom. *CATESOL Occasional Papers, California Association of Teachers of English to Speakers of Other Languages,* November 1–8.